C000263893

MG and Austin Healey SPRIDGETS

Chris Harvey

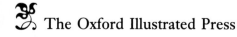 The Oxford Illustrated Press

© Chris Harvey and The Oxford Illustrated Press, 1983
Printed in Great Britain by J H Haynes & Co Limited
ISBN 0 902280 96 1
The Oxford Illustrated Press, Sparkford, Yeovil, Somerset, BA22 7JJ
Distributed in North America by Haynes Publications Inc,
861 Lawrence Drive, Newbury Park, California 91320

Contents

Acknowledgements

It's difficult to know where to start when you have to thank all the people who ever gave you a hand with a Spridget, let alone writing a book on them! My love affair with the cars started years ago when I managed to wheedle the oldest Frogeye I've ever seen out of a colleague, John Firth. Heartfelt thanks are due to Tony Amiss and Bob Needham for helping me to rebuild it in only three years . . . sad to say it had to be on its way during the financial recession of the 1970s, but not before I'd delved deep into their past with the help of none other than John Thornley, received the encouragement of Donald Healey, and gleaned much from conversations with Geoffrey Healey, Barrie Bilbie, Geoff Price and Fred Draper of the old Healey Motor Company, plus John Sprinzel who stands alone in the history of the Spridget. More than anybody could imagine was learned from nights drinking with John Chatham in Bristol, and days spent marvelling at the deep knowledge of Ron Gammons and Gerry Brown in Hertfordshire; from further nights spent drinking with Bill and Stephanie Barnett in Los Angeles; days and nights of encouragement from fellow Healey club members Dave Ramstad, Renee Cades, Ken Walsh, Bill and Betty Emerson on the West coast of America; not enough time with British Healey club members Derrick Ross, Ted Worswick and Carolyne Waters; support of every kind from Terry Grimwood and the invaluable help of Anders Clausager at British Leyland Heritage; Len and Bernard Bull of Monza Motors, Chris Maddock and Denise Grosvenor for supplying cars for special photography, plus pictures willingly provided by John Dunbar, Maurice Selden, Martin Elford, Stephen Tee, Gary Scott and Kathy Ager of London Art-Technical, my good friends Paul Skilleter and Bob Young, to supplement the Hilton Press Services ones my wife, Mary and I couldn't take. My thanks also to Mary for taking the news so well that I'd bought another Spridget, just as derelict if not more, as the first, and to Robin Ottaway of Bertram Cowan Motor Spares for concealing it until such time that I can sneak it out to restore it or turn it into a Westfield if that is impossible. My sincere thanks also to Jane Marshall and John Haynes for providing me with a vehicle—this book—to tell the story of the Spridgets. They are cars I just can't resist.

Chris Harvey,
London E8
December 1983

Colour Plates

I
The Cars They Called Spridgets

Donald Healey has to take the credit for inventing the Spridget though he was prompted by Leonard Lord, who had noticed that the demise of the MG Midget in 1955 had left a gap in the small sports car market. Healey knew that what Lord really wanted was not another MG, but an up-to-date sports version of the Austin Seven made by his firm before the war. Lord had no love for MG. They had sacked him once. So it was to be an Austin ... as austere as the Seven that had helped save Austin when they were down.

So Healey and his family, with a brilliant designer and chassis man, did what Austin's engineers had not the time for because they were wrestling with the Mini. In double quick time, the Healeys produced a prototype that was as near as they could make it a copy of the most inspiring sports car of the day, the Jaguar D type, already on its way to three wins in a row at Le Mans. The chief difference was that Healey's car used cheap Austin parts, was a lot smaller, and cost about sixpence in the pound as much.

No matter that their belt-and-braces engineering gave it a bodyshell with no boot lid because they were afraid it would be too floppy—the baggage could be stuffed through a hole behind the seats. No matter that it had hardly any interior appointments; all the more room to breathe in the fresh air that flowed in through its open top. No matter that its headlights sprouted from the bonnet like a frog's eyes because the Healey's couldn't close them at the right price; the Frogeye as it was soon called, almost winked at you, seeming to share a secret. No matter all of this—with its wonderful grinning radiator grille it looked downright happy. It was one of the cheapest cars on the road, but it didn't look as though it was because it was so rich in fun. The Sprite, as it was called, was the car for young people or anybody out to recapture their youth or make sure they did not lose it. With wonderful twitchy handling more like a racing car than the sedate saloon car it was based on, it had that same saloon's rugged reliability and fantastically frugal fuel consumption. In its first year of production, 1958, it was even a competitive racer at a fraction of the price of its rivals. No wonder it sold well, especially in America, where there was a market wide open for anything that was fun to drive.

Because you could remove the hood and make it a truly open car, not even the

The cheeky appeal of the first Spridget, the Frogeye, is well illustrated by its half-elliptical radiator grille and prominent headlights with a rounded bonnet.

advent of the revolutionary Mini—the first cheap saloon that could hold the road better than a sports car—could kill off the Sprite. It had virtually the same engine as the Mini, so the Sprite benefited from a tuning industry that sprang up around the two cars; there seemed to be no limit to the amount of power they could handle. These shops sold endless go-faster goodies to young impressionable customers, with the Sprite as the front-runner because you could fit all sorts of glass fibre panels to make it look truly different. Week by week, month by month, you could turn your Sprite into almost anything—even a Lotus Elite lookalike!

This was the shape shared with conspicuous success by the very hottest Sprites that ran in all the great road races and competitions of the day. The car was so versatile you could have used it for an international rally one day, the club treasure hunt immediately after, and then gone to work with nothing more than petrol added the day after that.

By 1961, the age of planned obsolescence was upon us, and Leonard Lord had retired and had been replaced by a man who invented something else: badge engineering. To keep rival franchises happy beneath the British Motor Corporation umbrella, George Harriman changed the badges and trim on his

Frogeyes also performed well and were adapted for all sorts of competitions. This works car has been fitted with wire wheels, disc brakes, hardtop, fog and spot lights, and number identity lamp on the scuttle, besides engine and transmission modifications in preparation for international rallying.

Frogeye's body was altered considerably for the MG Midget Mark I, although the sporting appeal remained...

cars and called one an Austin, one a Morris, one an MG and so on. For reasons of economy, the Austin Healey Sprite was produced by its ancient rivals, MG, in the world's biggest sports car factory at Abingdon. So when BMC decreed that it should be restyled with a luggage boot lid and a corporate front holding headlights in a proper position, an MG Midget was also built; just the same, save for the badges and a bit of trim. Hand on heart, BMC salespeople swore that the two cars were different. They even quoted mark numbers to prove it. The new Sprite was a mark two because there had been one before. The new Midget was nothing at all because it was brand new. Later the Midget was always one official mark behind: Mark Three Sprite, Mark Two Midget; just the same, but different numbers. And everybody called them Spridgets.

Throughout its life, the 80-inch wheelbase floorpan remained unchanged from the one the Healeys had got so right from the start. It kept down the cost of

The Spridget was gradually improved over the years, this 1964 example having been uprated with a robust 1,100 cc engine, more conventional rear springs, and an interior redesigned to incorporate wind-up windows and quarter lights in the face of competition from Triumph's Spitfire.

Eventually the Sprite received a 1,275-cc engine and various other improvements before it was phased out of production as the Austin Sprite in 1971.

change and you still sat only a foot from the ground even if the seats got thicker and the windows wound up to encroach a little on the cockpit space.

Back in '64, the Spridget got door locks (would you believe it?) because in 1962, it had acquired a rival only slightly more expensive. This was the Triumph Spitfire, which had not only door locks, but luxuries such as wind-up windows rather than sidescreens as well. The Spitfire had a very similar performance and what was thought at first to be far more advanced independent rear suspension. But it took only a sudden change in direction in a fast S-bend to tuck one wheel under and perhaps even lose control. Spridgets always behaved themselves much better and were superbly safe. If wasn't until Triumph got their suspension sorted out that BMC replied ... with an ashtray!

But the power race was on between these deadly rivals. The Spridget's glorious old A-series engine could trace its ancestry—by stroke—back to the

The Midget carried on in production with minor styling changes, including rounded rear wheel arches, on this 1973 model.

A major reconstruction, entailing the use of 'rubber' bumpers, had to be carried out in 1974 to meet new U.S. safety regulations. The engine was also changed for a 1,500-cc Triumph unit in what was the Midget's last fling.

pre-war Austin Seven. But it reached the limit of its practical development in 1966 on 1,275 cc. Still they roared on, with ultra-lightweight competition Spridgets making a mockery of far bigger sports cars in every form of club competition.

If the Spridget got softer with a convertible hood that took only 'a little while' to get up in a storm, rather than a long time, it was still the cheapest passport to fun for two, Spitfires included. The rip-roaring Mini-Cooper S that was faster (and cost more) seated four in a warmer environment and was a car that contained the sports car market—but it couldn't kill the Spridget. The last Cooper S rolled off the line in 1971 as the Spridget was just gathering its second wind (round the back of your neck). Planned obsolescence had even gone out of fashion by the time draconian changes to regulations governing its biggest market, America—and particularly California—forced the final facelift. Not even massive 'rubber' bumpers and a transplant of the Triumph Spitfire's engine because the A-series could go no further, stopped the Spridget.

The Healeys lost their development contract in the corporate muddle after

BMC became British Leyland, and with no Healeys in the background and no Sprites for sale after 1971, the Spridget name was lost and all the new cars were called Midgets. They kept on selling until the last one was made at Abingdon in 1979, when BL was on its knees from trying to sell saloon cars at a profit. It made money for a near-bankrupt empire, it created fun where there had been none for 355,888 first owners. If you assume, averaged out, that all Spridgets had eight owners by now, that makes 2,847,104 people who have bought one. My first one was number 13, registered on 21 May 1958. I knew some other Spridget owners and they all said the same thing: there will never be another car that was so much fun for so little money, so friendly, and so utterly dependable. Sad to say, seems there will never be another. That's why so many are treasured today, restored and rebuilt by enthusiasts all over the world.

II

The Famous Frogeye

Many influences were evident in the layout and appearance of the original Frogeye Sprite apart from the D type Jaguar which had inspired everybody in Britain including the Healey family and their body designer, Gerry Coker. In a manner time-honoured throughout the motor industry, when they had an engineering problem they often solved it not by original thought, but by looking at the cars being produced by their rivals and seeing how they coped. It was the only realistic attitude for a firm which could hardly afford the development on one-off specials, let alone the sort of multi-million pound or dollar project that is almost commonplace today.

Initially, the Healeys thought that they might be able to make the Sprite cheaper than anybody else by using the same body panels front and rear.

Garage owner Dick Shattock had been having some success selling RGS Atalanta specials with Britain's first glass fibre body, the front and rear moulds of which were taken in 1954 from the nose of an HWM Jaguar. The main problem with this idea was the headlights: it was all very well to mould them in at the front to a regulation height, but what did you do with the same moulds at the back? There was also the radiator intake to consider, but perhaps this could be tacked onto the front as a small extra moulding ... nevertheless, it was the headlights that caused the major problem, as illustrated by MG chief John Thornley's comment: 'We are so governed by regulations that you start designing a car by taking a pair of headlights and then hanging it on the back.' Colin Chapman, who had one of the most brilliantly inventive minds in the motor industry, had got over this problem on his Mark 9 sports racing car for the Le Mans 24-hour race in 1955 by having spotlights mounted on a swivel bar upside down beneath the bonnet. When the bonnet was opened at a pitstop just before darkness, the plan was to simply swivel up the lights and lock them in position, closing the bonnet behind them! This idea was outlawed, but it certainly gave Donald Healey food for thought. He considered that a good engineer should be able to design a cheap and effective system—probably by cables or rods—that could raise and lower the headlights effectively from the cockpit. In fact, he was so convinced that the idea was practical (and a great sales gimmick as well as being an economy factor), that he did not give in over the

The Frogeye, or Mark I, Sprite, as it appeared in May 1958 in left-hand-drive export form, equipped with 'optional' bumper and overriders. The indicators were combined with the sidelights low on the front wings, sharing the same transparent glass. This view of the car also shows its characteristic tail-up stance when lightly loaded at the back.

The underside of the Sprite was remarkably clean in construction, a fact which contributed to the car's relatively long life in view of the minimal protection applied at the factory—in common with most other cars produced at that time. The exposed brake lines and fuel tank can be seen clearly here, along with the seat runner reinforcing strips.

pop-up headlights until the cost of the linkage they had designed had to be balanced against the expensive nature of mounting a heavy steel bonnet at the front. Ironically, years later, Chapman was to resurrect the idea of cheaply-raised pop-up headlights on his Lotus Elan (originally conceived as a cheap glass fibre version of the Frogeye Sprite) by designing an ingenious system using manifold pressure.

Once the obvious decision had been taken to base the Sprite on Austin A35 components, the design of the floorpan was simple: it followed that of the D type

The rear suspension was of simple and robust design, although the rubber bushes used to insulate the floorpan from vibration were prone to produce some amazing squeaks if they dried out too much.

as far as was practical. The new car had to be made from steel to keep down costs—the thought of making a car's body and chassis entirely from glass fibre was a gleam only in Chapman's eye at that time.

Basically, chassis designer Barrie Bilbie laid down a punt-type floorpan on as short as possible a wheelbase—6 feet 8 inches. He could not make it any shorter and still find room for the occupants to sit with their legs outstretched, let alone leave sufficient length of propellor shaft to avoid problems with its universal joints and undue pressure being put on the gearbox end bearing by suspension movement. Keeping the wheelbase as short as possible had a number of advantages: it cut down on weight and the cost of raw materials; it made the floorpan stiffer because there was a shorter length of metal to twist; and it endowed the new car with incredibly agile handling. Against this had to be set a ride that would be choppy to say the least. But this did not seem a serious disadvantage at the time when sports cars were expected to be stiffly sprung and, as it happened, aroused no adverse comment from road testers for years.

The Sprite was the first car that Bilbie, and certainly the Healeys, had designed on a monocoque basis; and even though Geoffrey was good at stress calculations, they were worried about its stiffness. Monocoque construction was in its infancy at the time and they did not have the benefit of a fixed roof to provide vital stiffening. In fact, they considered themselves to be handicapped by having to provide quite large (24 inches wide) doors for their strong potential export market. This was a problem that Malcolm Sayer, the aerodynamicist who had designed the D type Jaguar did not have to contend with; racing drivers could simply leap through tiny hatches in the top of his aircraft-like body tub, leaving a far larger surrounding area of metal for stiffening. The tubular space frames employed on many sports racing cars at that time, including the Lotus Mark 9, were unsuitable because they cost too much to make in quantity. But

The instrument panel and interior were of exceptionally simple design, although all the instruments you needed for a sports car were there: from the left on this left-hand-drive car—fuel gauge, speedometer (incorporating mileometer and tripmeter), indicator warning light (which blinked with infuriating intensity in your eyes), rev counter, choke, combined oil pressure (top) and water temperature (bottom) gauge, windscreen wiper switch, separate ignition switch (which also worked the lights), with the indicator switch above it, heater, optional screen washer push-pull button, with the starter cable pull above it. Passengers were provided with a grab handle, and the driver with a large two-spoke steering wheel to hang on to. Trimming was kept to a minimum, the door frames and gearlever housing remaining in painted metal. Moulded rubber mats were fitted as standard, and there was only minimal clearance between the bottom of the instrument panel and the gear knob for people who liked to grip it with a clenched fist as they changed into first or third. The handbrake lever was situated on the left-hand side of the transmission tunnel on all cars, which could be very convenient for left-hand drivers, and frequently very amusing for right-hand drivers with passengers. Slots in the top of the scuttle between the trimming and the underside of the screen provided a primitive form of demisting from the heater (concealed behind the scuttle) which was either full on or full off.

Porsche were getting away with a platform-type chassis on their open Type 356 cars, so the Healeys decided that they could do the same.

The main problem as they saw it, was in mounting the rear suspension. If they used A35 running gear in its entirety, they would have to provide rear mounting points for its half-elliptic back springs. Geoffrey's calculations showed that a floorpan might have to be made unnecessarily heavy to accommodate them; Porsche did not have this problem because they had an entirely different and much more expensive torsion bar rear suspension, like that on the D type. It was a problem that had been causing a great deal of worry to the early designers of monocoque bodyshells, and Bill Heynes at Jaguar, for one, had taken the unusual step of using quarter elliptic rear springs—which had been hardly seen since before the war—at the back of his new Mark One saloon in 1955.

It was hardly surprising that the Healeys decided that this cheap and effective system would solve their problems by concentrating stresses locally within the wheelbase at the floorpan in front of the rear axle. The Jaguar saloons—which were starting to dominate saloon car racing at the time the Sprite was being designed—could be made to handle sufficiently well with a great deal more power, so the Healeys opted for quarter elliptics. The idea of a Panhard rod like that used on the Jaguar Mark One was rejected as an unnecessary complication in view of the much lower weight and power output of the Sprite, allied to the fact that they could use relatively stiff springs for extra location because it was a sports car.

The platform chassis that resulted was of almost pure Jaguar D type and Porsche 356 concept, terminating at the front in a very rigid boxed scuttle with an upswept pan over the rear axle replacing the Jaguar's rear bulkhead. Like the

D type, but on a smaller scale, the floor pan was reinforced by boxed sill structures—but still of no less than five inches depth—with a tunnel in the middle fully enclosing the propellor shaft as a stiff backbone. Further reinforcing 'top-hat' sections were welded above the rear suspension mountings in front of the axle to spread their stress. Strong steel inner wheelarches helped support the luggage boot floor and complete the tail section, which when welded together formed a strong box that had only an opening behind the seats to compromise rigidity (and accept luggage!).

Jaguars had calculated that they could no longer fit a sunroof to their Mark One saloon—as they had on earlier models—because it would cost too much in rigidity. The Healeys transferred this philosophy to the top panel in their tail, and at the same time dispensed with the expense and inconvenience of providing a boot lid and sealing! It must be remembered that at the time the Sprite was being designed, MG had only just stopped making the T series with no luggage boot at all and many fans of cheap sports cars were still used to carrying their luggage either stuffed behind the seats or on a rack at the back. In such circumstances, the Sprite's lack of a luggage boot lid seemed a fair compromise. It also offered the further advantage that with no bulkhead to provide between the seats and the luggage area—which would have been needed with a lid— relatively long items of baggage could be accommodated from within. To put it

The rear end of the Sprite was equally simple in construction, being made up of a pressing with wings welded on each side. Rearlights and stoplights shared the top red lenses, with amber glass for the indicators beneath because it was illegal to show a white light at the rear in Britain. Petrol reached the tank beneath the luggage boot floor through a long rubber pipe from the filler. Small optional overriders were fitted for vestigial protection, rather than a full width bumper bar, to save money and because the Healeys had hoped to have either a hatch for the spare wheel, or a partly-exposed wheel to act as a buffer, in place of the number plate indentation. Such luxuries were ruled out for economy in production.

Roughly-cut leatherette trimmed the bottom of the boot, into which all sorts of objects, notably the spare wheel, could be inserted. If they were small, however, there was a possibility that they might be lost for ever!

another way, if it was the right shape, you could stow nearly twice as much in the back of a Sprite as you might have done otherwise in one of its rivals.

A fuel tank of only six gallons was slung beneath the luggage boot floor. A bigger tank would have meant having to provide more solid mountings, and more important, the extra weight of fuel it could hold might have had an unbalancing effect on such a short car. The spare wheel also had to live in the tail, but inside the boot, where—even if it was difficult to remove and return—it stayed clean.

At the front, the entire bonnet, wings, radiator grille and headlamp assembly formed a steel unit just like that of the Jaguar D type. But unlike the Jaguar with its alloy bonnet, the Sprite's had to be made from steel, so it was very heavy. This meant that the only economical place to hinge it was at the scuttle—hence the problem with the pop-up headlights. In an almost 'productionised' version of the Jaguar system, two box-section girders extended forward from a crossmember in the floorpan on a line with the front of the doors (and the back of the scuttle), that was, in turn, linked to top hat sections running back to the rear suspension mountings. Braces either side of the scuttle absorbed some of the front suspension stresses. Inner wheelarches were fitted alongside from the front of large boxes around the occupants' legs. These boxes were also welded to the tops of the sills, which swept up from the front of the scuttle. Everything was held together at the front of the chassis by a very substantial boxed structure, which included a wide crossmember to carry the suspension and steering and further bracing for the tops of the suspension mountings. The front of the bonnet rested on the extended engine legs, locked by a twist-grip handle.

When Austin's production engineers first examined the Sprite's prototype built by the Healey Motor Company, they thought they could switch to the thinner metal used on the A35—but this cracked up around the rear suspension mountings and thankfully they reverted to the steel specified by the Healeys, with some additional gussets.

The bonnet opened up like an alligator's mouth and there was a
distinct risk that the unwary might
be gobbled up if he or she forgot to
fix the security stay in place. This car
has been fitted with air horns, oil
cooler and rubber straps on the
chassis legs to help hold down the
bonnet at speed.

When they left the factory, Frogeye
Sprites were fitted with a collapsible
support (on the right of the picture)
to hold up the bonnet, with an
additional stay (on the left) that had
to be clipped in place to make sure
the bonnet did not fall. This example shows the original position for
the ignition coil on top of the
dynamo, with air intake trunking
leading from a position beside the
radiator, to the optional heater,
mounted high in front of the heater.
The windscreen washers, also optional, have their nozzles mounted
close together on the scuttle top,
with their reservoir low on the right-
hand side of the radiator when
viewed from the front of the car.

The Austin A35's front suspension was lifted direct onto the Sprite with special steering arms to adapt it for use with the Morris Minor's rack, seen to the left in front of the suspension. This system endowed every Sprite with very responsive steering and went a long way to establishing the character of the car.

Using the A35's running gear was not quite so simple as it might have seemed. The rear axle was about the right width, so its track of 3 ft 8.75 ins, with standard 5.20-13 pressed steel wheels, was adopted. After a considerable amount of experimentation on this prototype, and a second built with the thinner metal, the final way of adapting this normally half-elliptic sprung axle to quarter elliptic operation was devised. Brackets were welded to the back of the axle casing to take, at the bottom, the eyes of the 15-leaf springs. They were then anchored firmly at the other end to the floorpan, with reinforcing plates underneath. The tops of the brackets behind the axle provided a pivot point for a parallel arm above each spring, to relieve it of torque stresses. The spring itself still had to cope with most of the lateral forces of cornering, however.

The radius arms, and the spring eyes, were mounted in rubber bushes to cut noise, vibration, and maintenance. The tops of the reinforcing boxes in front of the axle fairing provided the second mounting for the radius arms, with restraint straps to stop the axle dropping too far on rebound, and rubber bump stops at the tops of the axle brackets. Two more brackets were welded in front of the axle to take links which, in turn, worked Armstrong lever arm dampers bolted to gussets in the axle fairing. Telescopic shock absorbers were more efficient, but the old-fashioned lever arm dampers were preferred because in this position they localized stressed around the suspension mountings and did not need separate and costly towers above the axle line. In any case, they were still in wide use at that time and were the same as those used in the front suspension. This came direct from the A35 with pressed steel lower wishbones and forged upper links which also formed the arms of its shock absorbers. The upper and lower links were of unequal length to minimize track variations—the actual track at rest being 3 ft 9.75 ins. Coil springs provided the suspension medium.

The BMC A-series power train in the original form fitted to the Sprite, with its oil filter beneath the dynamo, close to the starter motor, which nestles under the distributor. The clutch release and gearbox side plate can be seen just behind the starter. The gearlever had to be as long as it was—with the risk of barking the drivers' knuckles under the instrument panel—to provide enough leverage for proper working of its long extension on top of the gearbox.

Carburettors and exhaust were fitted on the other side of the engine, separated by a heat shield. The radiator filler cap was kept well out of the way of the ignition coil! The tap just visible in front of the heater, at the back of the cylinder block, cut off supplies of hot water from the head to the heater's radiator in warm weather, letting through cool draughts via the air trunking to the left. Fumes from the crankcase were piped, from a position next to the oil filler, out through one of the carburettor's air cleaners.

The standard A35 steering was appalling, however, the play necessary for smooth operation of its box, idler, and six ball joints making it feel downright sloppy in the short-wheelbase Sprite. Most of the British sports racing cars, such as the products of Lotus, were using the excellent Morris Minor rack and pinion steering gear, so the Healeys tried this in conjunction with special steering arms to link it with the rest of the A35 suspension. There was no problem about using Morris parts, because, with the merger of Austin and Morris to form BMC in 1952, they now came out of the same corporate parts bin, and—although relatively expensive in itself—the rack and pinion unit cost only about the same as all the Austin bits and pieces it replaced. Even when fitted with a 16-inch steering wheel of the size fashionable at the time, the new steering gear, needing only 2.33 turns from lock to lock, endowed the Sprite with the almost miraculous responsiveness that was to characterise Spridgets throughout their production life.

The A35's mechanical back brakes were hardly any better than its steering, and presented problems on the Sprite with only five inches of ground clearance, so once again the Morris Minor came to the rescue. Its 7-inch drum brakes, made by Lockheed, were grafted on to produce an effective means of stopping the new cars, with a hydraulic system filched from the MGA sports car. Again there was no problem; it all came out of the BMC store.

The A35 and its rival, the Morris Minor 1000, used the same basic power train, BMC's A-series engine and gearbox. But even in the Minor's slightly more powerful installation with an SU carburettor, it did not produce enough power to give the Sprite a decent sports car performance. But these units were already widely used in competition, so Healeys cobbled up a twin SU set up like that used on the MGA for evaluation on their prototype while BMC decided what to do about it in production. A wide range of ratios were available for the A35 final drive, so a 4.22:1 was selected to give the car 15.4 mph per 1000 rpm in conjunction with the standard A-series gearbox. The overall ratios that resulted from this combination were, first, 15.31, second 10.02, third 5.96 and top 4.22, with a 19.62 reverse—rather large gaps in the best stump-pulling saloon car tradition, but acceptable because the engine had plenty of torque. The lack of synchromesh on first gear was quite normal at the time. It saved money and the straight cut first gears were stronger in any case. Besides, there was still a large percentage of motorists who prided themselves on silent changes with 'crash' gearboxes, expecially those keen on sports cars. There was also a firm climate of opinion at that time that four forward gears were enough: Ford, for instance, was still fitting a three-speed gearbox on its small cars, a configuration that was still overwhelmingly popular in the United States. As a result, no provision was made for fitting an overdrive, which would have been an expensive option in any case. The Healeys were quite rightly concentrating on producing a very cheap and basic car, so the transmission tunnel was made as narrow as possible. This meant that it did not infringe more than necessary on the occupants' legroom.

Although the new car was essentially a project for Austin production and

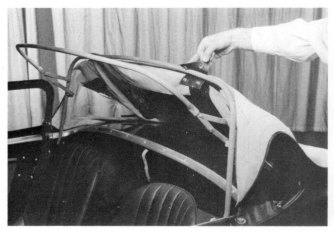

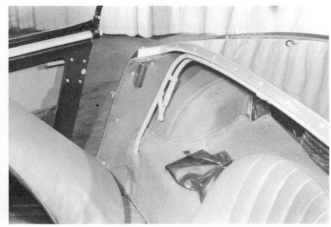

The hood was attached by a simple folding frame plugged into tubes behind the seats, with its material held down by press studs at the back, top, and on the windscreen rail. The fabric was tensioned when the front support was swung up to the position shown in the first picture. When the hood was folded, it would be stored in the boot, with or without the sidescreens, the folding frame being held in place in the front of the luggage boot entrance by the strap dangling from the centre of the tail pressing. In the picture with one seat folded forward, the door release catch can just be seen, ready to poke the unwary in the elbow. The dark-coloured satchet lying on the axle casing behind the seats contained essential tools, such as the jack.

distribution, it wound up with their erstwhile rivals, Morris, doing much of the development! This was because it would have need a lot of redesigning for production on the Austin A35 lines at Longbridge, Birmingham, where the power trains were inserted into the body units from underneath. Because of the shape of the Sprite's chassis legs, the engine had to be lowered onto them; if the legs had been reshaped to accept the engine from underneath, they would have made the car too wide in this instance. In any case, Longbridge was being cleared at that time for production of the new Mini, so the Sprite was sent down to the MG works at Abingdon for assembly alongside its 'big sister', the Austin-Healey 100-Six. MG, of course, was an offshoot of the original Morris empire which had merged with Austin. The Mini—with its transmission running in the same oil as its A-series engine—presented more than enough problems for Austin's engine men, so work to extract more reliable power for the Sprite installation was transferred to the old Morris engines department at Courthouse Green, Coventry.

Even then the A-series engine had a long history. It could be seen as a natural evolution of Austin's 1200 cc small car unit that was introduced in 1947. A four-cylinder in-line unit, it had a three-bearing crankshaft running in thin-

Frogeye Sprite owners frequently attached 'racing mirrors' with wide-based, fared-in, mountings, to reduce image-distorting vibrations on the wing tops, and a luggage rack to carry what they couldn't stuff into the boot...

Others fitted a hardtop to stay snug in winter and wire wheels for appearance's sake (or to help ventilate overworked drum brakes), and if they could afford it, disc brakes to cure all the problems.

wall bearings, the first British production engine to do so when it appeared in 803 cc form for the new Austin Seven—or A30—in October 1951. This all-cast-iron engine had water jackets running the full length of the bores. So far as dimensions were concerned, it was slightly more modern than the original Austin Seven unit of pre-war fame in that it had a 2 mm wider bore at 58 mm, although it retained the same long stroke of 76 mm. This was a relic of the days when British cars' taxation was governed by the size of their bores, but at least it gave the A-series unit a lot of torque.

It was decided to put the camshaft, pushrods, inlet and exhaust valves on one side of the engine, so that the pushrod tubes did not have to pass the sparking plugs, which might be a source of oil and water leaks. This meant that the inlet ports had to be siamesed in the cylinder head with a siamesed central exhaust port. One side effect of this layout was that it put heavy demands on the exhaust valves and made the use of very high quality steel essential. But it was a very efficient cylinder head that had been developed by the legendary Harry Weslake. He discovered in wartime experiments with gasflow that a heart-shaped combustion chamber with a projection between inlet and exhaust valves promoted just the right degree of swirl to ensure complete combustion of the mixture. This Weslake-patented design also gave very smooth and economical part-throttle running on a small ignition advance.

The camshaft was driven by a roller chain from the crankshaft, with twin rubber tensioners. At the rear end of the camshaft there was an oil pump and at the front of the engine the water pump, driven by a belt from the crankshaft, that also drove the dynamo. Production was simplified by the use of a split connecting rod little end which clamped on to the gudgeon pin. This meant that any pin which fell within the design tolerance would fit.

More than 500,000 of these engines had been made by the time BMC

A sample from a day's production of Sprites is parked outside the factory at Abingdon, flanked by an Austin Healey 100-Six and an MG Magnette saloon ... with a Sprite sold to journalist John Anstice-Brown of *The Motor* in the foreground. He reported in the issue of 16 May 1960: 'Ownership of one of these cars started for me when I asked Marcus Chambers of the BMC Competitions Department one Friday what the chances were of a Sprite on the following Monday so that I could enter it in an Irish road race to be held in three weeks' time. They were, he assured me, quite definitely nil, but miracles do happen and once again the optimist was in luck and a car was ready for collection not on the Monday I had requested, but on the one after that, leaving very little time for preparation before we set sail for the Emerald Isle. With help from many friends, Speedwell modifications were hastily added, the headlights brutally chiselled off, tubes put into the tyres, and harder Mintex brake linings fitted, all in the space of four days during which the hours of nine to five were booked by less agreeable activities than fiddling with sports cars. Much to the amazement of one and all, the race provided the first win for a Sprite!'

started to develop it for further applications in 1956. In its initial single carburettor form, it produced only 36 bhp and more than 40 bhp was needed for the Sprite. This meant that it would have to have a larger capacity if it was to remain reasonably docile. The 803 cc engine had water all round its bores and its enlargement to 948 cc—originally visualised as the size needed to power the Mini—was undertaken with some trepidation because it meant siamesing the end pairs of cylinders. Early fears that bore distortion would result appeared to be well founded until it was discovered that a thick copper asbestos gasket was to blame and the problem could be cured by using a gasket of about half the thickness, 0.031 ins. White metal big end bearings had also proved to be a weak spot on the 803 cc unit, so they were changed for the same lead indium as the main bearings in the 948, which, in turn, led to a change from a by-pass to a full-flow filter. The big end journal diameter was also increased by 0.0625 ins to 1.625 ins, and 0.125 ins was taken off the main bearing length and used to thicken the crankshaft webs. These changes were enough to cope with up to 70 bhp from the A-series engine, which now used a bore of 62.94 mm with the same stroke as before. In its Sprite form, it had an 8.3:1 compression ratio, 1.0936-inch inlet valves, 1 inch stellite-faced exhaust valves and twin 1.125-inch SU carburettors, producing 42.5 bhp at 5,000 rpm with 52 lb/ft of torque at 3,300 rpm. Stronger valve springs had to be fitted, too, and the standard 6.25-inch Borg and Beck single dry plate clutch also received more powerful springs. Normally it had been operated mechanically, but because the MG master cylinder was used for the braking system, it could now be given hydraulic operation. In this application, the A-series engine was to prove outstandingly strong and economical and capable of taking a lot of tuning gear without protest.

One of the best-made hardtops that could be fitted to the Sprite was a rather bulbous affair sold by Ashley Laminates, which had the advantage of providing a certain amount of space for soft objects in the area under the rear window's lip and top of the tail. It was quite aerodynamic and often combined with a convenient hatch for spare wheel removal, based on that fitted as standard to the contemporary Triumph TR, and secured by the same car's coachlock. The main problem with this hardtop and others before sliding sidescreens were marketed, was that the only way into the car once the doors had been shut, was by forcing a hand between the trailing lip of the sidescreen and the hard edge of the top. The sidescreens lasted longer if you used a piece of wire ... but you sometimes had difficulty convincing interested onlookers that you were entitled to enter the Sprite by such means!

A few problems occurred with its installation in the Sprite that were chiefly electrical. The battery had to be located on the scuttle (not even BMC visualized anybody being able to service it in the boot!), which meant that it was shrouded by the rear-mounted bonnet; and the rear-mounted oil pump precluded the use of a normal rev counter drive. Smith's Instruments came to the rescue with a neat little gearbox drive for the rev counter, off the back of the dynamo.

During the year of development before its introduction on 20 May 1958, the Sprite received a number of detail improvements. External door hinges like those which were to be used on the Mini were thought to be the cheapest thing imaginable and highly attractive as a result. But Les Ireland, who had taken over

Other Sprites were far more extensively modified, including this works model with front-clamped hardtop, wire wheels, disc brakes, anti-roll bar, and special engine, gearbox and rear axle.

Hardtops came in a variety of styles, including this distinctly period version with moulded-in rain gutters. It is also interesting to note that this car has been fitted with the neat bonnet handles from a Triumph Spitfire to help keep the nose in place.

from Coker (who had left to work in the United States) discovered that two concealed hinges could be made as cheaply, so they were used and resulted in a vast improvement in appearance.

Despite the short wheelbase—only an inch longer than that of the A35, in which the occupants sat vertically, rather than stretched out horizontally as in the Sprite—the cockpit was roomier than that of the recently-designed MGA, which was one step up in the sports car world. This was because of the simple design of the body with its relatively sparse interior. Within an overall width of 4 ft 5.25 ins, no less than 4 ft 4.75 ins was available for the interior! The doors needed only 0.5 ins between them because they did not have to contain window winders or remote door handle mechanisms. The Sprite had sidescreens mounted on top of the doors with thumbscrews in the grand old manner. Cutouts in the door interiors meant to act as map pockets were so large that the occupants could genuinely use all the space for elbow room, providing they didn't hack themselves on tiny door handles that protruded forward from the back. No exterior door handles were fitted—you just slipped your hand between the sidescreen and the hood, and opened the door that way—whether or not you were entitled to do so. In those days, sports cars were used with their hoods down far more often than nowadays, partly because cheap ones such as the Sprite had flat windscreens, that—although they did nothing for their performance aerodynamically—deflected the slipstream right over the occupants' heads, rather than whipping it round the backs of their necks as today's more streamlined screens are prone to do. Rain went right over the top when the car was travelling reasonably quickly, too, and it was likely to be doing that for a longer time than today because there was less traffic on the road. A third factor that opted for more open-air driving was the fact that fewer people had central heating in those days and the average man or woman was used to wearing more clothing—particularly overcoats—so they did not object so much to riding in an open car, and did not wonder why it was not fitted with a heater as standard. The Sprite's was optional, as was the front bumper, officially. But few left the factory without such fittings—it was simply a widely-used ruse for putting up the advertised price with compulsory extras. The total absence of locks and so on— even an ashtray in the days when far more people smoked—was one of the reasons the Sprite's cost could be kept so low. Geoffrey Healey, a regular smoker, did most of the early road testing, flicking his ash out of the driver's side. ...

A rare sight today ... the original Peasmarsh bonnet, which used fared-in headlights and the standard grille.

Another reason for the Sprite's relative roominess within an overall length of only 11 ft (without front bumper; 5 ins more with it in place) was that the trim was so spartan, seats included. These were an object lesson in design—being based on the Big Healey's frames—in how to locate the occupants firmly and comfortably within a bucket shape. It was only years later when seats became thicker for a plush appearance that the Sprite started to feel really cramped. Even with the simple hood erected to an overall height of 4 ft 1.75 ins, there was 3 ft 1.5 ins of head room because there was nothing more than a sheet of canvas—or PVC-coated fabric in reality—above and the thickness (or thinness some would have said) of the seat mounted on the floor beneath you.

With such well-tried mechanical components, there was little that needed changing during the Frogeye's production run; just the original hood, which showed a woeful lack of development in that it didn't fit properly at the top of the windscreen. It looked quite all right while the car was standing in the showrrom, but as soon as it was driven at speed, the material raised to such an extent that bugs, rain and road debris sailed straight through the gap at the top of the screen and hit the occupants full in their faces! This deficiency was soon rectified with a steel strip being fitted into the front of the material so that it could be slotted into a revised windscreen top rail. The door handles were also fitted with protective knobs at the same time, and the ignition coil, which had a habit of vibrating itself apart on top of the dynamo, was moved to a more secure place a few inches away on the adjacent inner front wing.

No sooner had the Sprite been introduced than specialised tuning firms got to work on it; it was a dream come true for them as a basic car that could take all sorts of accessories, stage by stage. Speedwell conversions, started their partnership with A35 racer John Sprinzel and world champion-to-be Graham Hill, and were one of the first in this field with a hardtop for the Sprite in July 1958. This relatively expensive option—priced at around £50—had a number of advantages: its rigid shape offered better aerodynamics and, in conjunction with Speedwell exterior door handles, made the car less vulnerable to thieves and vandals. A majority of buyers opted for hardtops, however, on the assumption that they would make the car quieter and more refined, as well as being more weatherproof; this was not entirely the case as the standard hood did a perfectly good job, (once it had been de-bugged) of keeping the car snug, and the hardtops made the interior far noisier, their glass fibre construction acting like the skins of a drum! They also required the fitting of more sophisticated sidescreens, not the standard solid type. Some other way had to be devised to find a strong and unyielding hardtop. So sidescreens with sliding portions were made at considerable expense: £12.50 a pair. But such was the convenience of the sliding screens, particularly for providing instant ventilation from within— you had to remove the standard ones entirely to let in any air—that they eventually became normal wear on Sprites.

Universal Laminations made the first Speedwell hardtops with a shape that followed the lines of the normal hood, but a back window even larger, a wraparound affair inspired by that of the long-defunct Austin A90 Atlantic. This PVC-covered hardtop was soon followed by others, with those moulded by Ashley as the most ambitious. The Ashley hardtop was a bulbous affair that had

Early Speedwell bonnets also had fared-in headlights beneath Perspex covers, with a shape and small air intake based on the nose of the racing Lotus Elite. They also had pronounced swage lines on the sides. As with the Peasmarsh bonnet, the headlights stayed at a universally-legal height.

an almost hunchbacked, but highly aerodynamic, shape which extended well down the tail of the car. It offered a lot more interior space and was of such impressive design and quality that it also made the car a lot more civilised inside. But the most popular hardtop was that made by the works, which had been designed at Abingdon along the lines of the normal hood, but with a slightly smaller rear window for extra rigidity. This hardtop clamped to the top of the windscreen with prominent chrome-plated clips.

Tuners were equally quick off the mark with engine conversions for the Sprite, many as the result of experience in making the A35 and Morris Minor go faster. Front runners included Downton Engineering, who could supply a kit comprising a gas-flowed cylinder head with compression ratios varying between 10.3:1 and 12:1 (if you fitted flat-topped pistons), that when combined with larger carburettors and special manifolds, would give a Sprite from 92 mph to nearly 100 ... all for £100 or so. Throughout the life of the Sprite, Downtons were among the best, with early competition from firms such as hill climber Michael Christie's Alexander Engineering.

The sheer weight—72 lb—of the steel bonnet and its unusual appearance led to a variety of glass fibre bonnets being offered, usually based on the beautiful Lotus Elite, which had its headlamps mounted conventionally in the front wings. In most cases these bonnets weighed about half as much as the steel

Later Speedwell bonnets used the same basic lines, but had lower inset headlights so lighting efficiency was not impaired and drag was reduced. The headlight height was too low for some countries, however. These bonnets were also hinged at the front, rather than the back, and secured with small inset side clips, beneath flat sides unbroken by a swage line.

Speedwell also marketed a far more aerodynamic hardtop based on the roof of a Sebring Sprite, that was moulded to the body with an integral replacement windscreen. This car has been fitted with their popular exterior door handles that linked to the normal catch inside through a slot in the door skin, and the longer nose Monza bonnet.

one and cost about the same as a hardtop. But the first off the mark was the Peasmarsh, made in Guildford to a design that owed a lot to the small Berkeley sports car built by a caravan manufacturer. This bonnet had the market almost entirely to itself for a year from its introduction early in 1959 until Speedwell hired aerodynamicist Frank Costin, who had worked on the Elite, to improve their competition cars. Speedwell had spectacular success at Sebring, so these Elite-style bonnets became known as Sebring Sprite bonnets. They were widely copied until Ashley trounced everybody in December 1960 with a bonnet that made the Sprite look like a miniature Ferrari—for the first time it had a completely different grille—but was, in fact, based on the ill-fated pioneer British glass fibre-bodied car, the Jowett Jupiter R4 of 1953.

The Healey Motor Company were also prominent in this market, chiefly selling front anti-roll bars which had been developed to improve handling during the Sprite's prototype stage, and woodrim steering wheels that were eventually to become the preserve of firms such as Speedwell and Les Leston's motor accessories. They also listed disc brake and wire wheel conversions that were not only expensive at around £100, but difficult to obtain unless you were a top-line racer. For a while, they also marketed a Shorrock supercharger kit that, in theory, was far superior to the normal methods of producing extra horsepower and torque but did not always work so well in practice—and suffered from bitter opposition among the insurance companies.

In this way the Sprite progressed through the first three years of its life with a whole new industry springing up around it, selling extras to conversions that were sufficiently extensive to almost make it into a completely different car.

III

The Chrome-Front Spridgets

Special bonnets for Sprites had achieved such popularity by 1960 that BMC began to wonder if they ought to change the car's shape, particularly as it had no luggage lid. The American philosophy of planned obsolescence was reaching its height then, so it needed only a drop in sales from 21,566 in 1959 to 18,665 in 1960 to reinforce their opinions. In any case, they thought: if people are willing to spend so much money on changing the appearance of a Sprite, why not do it for them and cream off the profits made in the accessory business? So BMC asked the Healeys to design a new front end along strict guidelines: it had to have the headlights in the wings and feature a separate bonnet. The advantage of such a bonnet, the marketing men pointed out, was that it would be lighter to lift and as a result prove more attractive to women. The all-enveloping bonnet might appear to offer better access, but headroom was so limited this was not entirely the case in practice. Naturally, the Healeys were told to keep quiet about what BMC were planning to do. At the same time, Syd Enever was finalising plans on the MGB to replace BMC's medium-sized sports car, the MGA. This had a separate luggage boot in a squared-off tail, so it seemed a simple matter to see if it could be adapted for use on the Sprite, particularly as it was planned to produce the Sprite as an MG as well. Well aware of the machinations of the BMC management mind, Enever and Thornley decided to check what the Healeys were up to ...

The result was that the two parties got together to blend in the new front and rear halves of the Spridget-to-be! As it turned out, the front end bore some resemblance to the Ashley bonnet so far as its lines were concerned, and more than a passing relationship to the new MGB. The rear end was also distinctly like that of the MGB, but on a smaller scale. The Healey's prototype (complete with a Frogeye rear end) featured a trendy bonnet air scoop that was rejected on ground of cost, but found its way onto Speedwell's demonstrator after the new model came out. Part of Enever's redesign of the rear end included a conversion to half-elliptic springs, his work in this area on the Big Healey having been particularly successful in turning it into a top-line rally car. The same system was to be used on the MGB, but it was rejected—again on the grounds of cost—on the Sprite, although the difference must have been marginal as the tail that

The new panels used on the first Spridgets fitted neatly on top of the existing floorpan and incorporated the original doors and scuttle. This is an MG Midget with its chrome radiator grille, and strips along the sides and bonnet centre. It is fitted with a works outside-clamp hardtop.

Rear view of the MG Midget showing its revised tail with outside luggage boot lid, vertical handle and neat works hardtop that had a glass window (rather than the more common plastic), for better visibility. It also cost more than most proprietory makes ... Octagonal badges appeared all over the new Midget, including one in the centre of the boot lid, but surprisingly, not on the hub caps. The A-H logo also disappeared from the Sprite's hub caps at this time, in the interests of economical production. Until the very last minute before introduction, it had been intended to use Frogeye-type rear overriders, but the U.S. marketing men managed to convince BMC that a rear bumper bar like that fitted to the front would be more attractive to potential customers and help keep insurance premiums down. As a result, the original mounting holes that had been provided in the new rear panel were blanked off with chrome plates.

went into production included extended box sections which would form the basis for half-elliptic rear mountings. But suspension was something you couldn't see at first glance in the showroom and production pennies were considered better spent on appearance. Inevitably, however, the extra weight of the new rear end made the quarter elliptic Spridgets even twitchier, but you should have tried telling that to a marketing man of the Sixties ...

Both the Healeys and various tuners had tried cutting away the area behind the seats as far back as the hood line, so that large objects could be packed there, but now the marketing men took inspiration from the Triumph TR and offered a cushion for the rear platform in the forlorn hope that they could convince potential customers that the Sprite could accommodate more than two people. It was a ruse that worked well for Triumph, with a slightly bigger car, but it was

The Healey family continued to market the original MG-designed and Jensen-built hardtop for the Sprite, with its distinctive oval rear window and small quarter lights.

BMC took a leaf out of Triumph's book and made a 'rear seat' for the Spridget—but they did not sell many because there was hardly room for anybody's legs and precious little for their head either. Oddly enough, the same idea in the Triumph TR had sold quite well despite similar restrictions on space! One of the optional 'Rimbellisher' wheeltrims that were popular fittings to Spridgets at the time, can be seen at the bottom right-hand side of the picture.

Seat belt mountings were also fitted to Spridgets for the first time, with one anchorage either side of the transmission tunnel and the others on top of each rear wheelarch—but it would be years before seat belts would be fitted as standard, and then only when they became compulsory. The car in the picture is a Sprite, with its odd mixture of carpet on vertical rear surfaces and seat backs, and ribbed rubber on horizontal and transmission tunnel sides.

hardly surprising that the Sprite's optional back seat proved unattractive! There was only three inches of adjustment on the driver's seat and none at all in basic form for the passenger.

Structurally, Enever's new rear end used reinforced wing sides, squared-off arches, and a strongly-lipped boot aperture to avoid having to rely on a heavy bulkhead between the cockpit and the boot. Until the very last moment, the Mark II Sprite prototypes were fitted with Frogeye over-riders, before these were replaced by a bumper to match the new one at the front. Overall length was hardly any more, however, at 11 ft 4 ins. Outwardly, the front-end conversion was as delightfully simple in construction as the engineering that had characterised the Frogeye. New wings simply bolted on over the existing sills, with a new bonnet, grille and front apron filling the gap in between. Inwardly, it looked more complex, but in reality all that was done was to substitute new wheelarches—the scuttle and doors remaining unchanged.

The overall weight went up 59 lb to 1,525 lb and the blunt front end did not prove to be so aerodynamic as the first bonnet, even with its frog's eyes. So more power was needed. This was achieved along the lines exploited by several tuners: the cylinder head was revised to give a 9:1 compression ratio—now that high-octane petrol was available almost anywhere—and better breathing was obtained by using a higher-overlap camshaft and larger inlet valves. With the

The underbonnet layout of the Spridget was much the same as that of the Frogeye, with only the odd change. The carburettors have received pancake air filters and the screenwashers are still optional.

Advertising agencies were still rather naive in the early 1960s. The popular image of the sports car that they wished to project was one of young blood dashing down to the pub with some bird in tow ... ignoring the perils associated with alcohol. Imagine the furore today of any car, let alone a 'high performance' one, being connected so closely with a pint!

new camshaft, the inlets opened 5 degrees before top dead centre and closed 45 degrees after bottom dead centre as before, but the exhaust opening was put forward from 40 degrees to 51 degrees before bottom dead centre and closure delayed from 10 degrees to 21 degrees after top dead centre, thus giving an increase in overlap from 15 degress to 26 degrees. The new inlet valves had been increased in diameter by 0.0625 ins to 1.156 ins, the exhausts remaining at 1 inch. Double, instead of single, valve springs were used. Larger 1.25-inch SU HS2 carburettors had Coopers paper element air cleaners, complete with cool-air intakes. The latest distributor, with steel rolling weights to reduce friction, was fitted. In this form, the engine did not produce much more power (only 46.2 bhp at 5,500 rpm) and almost exactly the same torque, 52.5 lb/ft, but the torque peaked at 2,750 rpm instead of 3,300.

This meant that it was so much more flexible that the close-ratio gearbox which had been a competition option was deemed suitable for standard use. Its ratios went a long way to filling in the gap between second and third, with first notably higher as well. The new ratios were, first 3.2 (against 3.63), second 1.92 (2.37), third 1.36 (1.41), fourth 1.00 (1.00) with a 4.11 (4.66) reverse.

Amazingly, the bumpers—without which a car never left the factory—were still listed as an option, along with such extras as a radio, heater, windscreen washers, rev counter (again a standard fitting in reality), tonneau cover and supporting rail, laminated competition windscreen, locking petrol cap, cigarette lighter, wing-mounted mirrors, wheel discs, hardtop, whitewall tyres, twin horns, luggage carrier and adjustable passenger's seat. Of these, the front and rear bumpers, with over-riders, screen washers, rev counter and adjustable passenger's seat were standard fittings on a de luxe model—but never an ash tray! Part of the rear-end redesign included seat belt mountings, however.

At the end of the month of introduction for the Sprite Mark II, in June 1961, the first MG Midget since the T series was replaced by the MGA, made

'Lift mat to fill' said the legend stamped on the rubber mat at the side of the gearbox housing. The floppy rubber covering did not last long and was soon replaced by assorted pieces of carpet by most owners.

its appearance. This was a classic example of badge engineering in that it was almost exactly the same as the de luxe version of the Sprite—and very few bog standard Sprites were made! For an extra £10, customers could have horizontal chrome strips along each side, and another one along the centre line of the bonnet, a full complement of octagons, and a grille with vertical slats—the traditional sign of a more expensive car—instead of the Mark II Sprite's horizontal aluminium mesh. The interior was also a good deal different, with seat covering more like that of the MGA (including contrasting piping), a leatherette-covered dashboard with padded rail, and white plastic steering wheel that reeked of transatlantic influence. The new Midget shared the same toggle switches as the Sprite, but, for some curious reason, had far clearer markings on its instrument faces. It also had better quality floor covering. Sliding sidescreens had been standardised in conjunction with those on the Sprite, but to make matters more confusing, the MG was offered with a different optional hardtop. This was made at Abingdon, whereas the previous one had been produced by Jensens to an MG design and continued to be offered for the Sprite. The new hardtop was readily distinguishable by its squarer lines, but more important, it had a glass rear window for vastly improved vision.

Sad to see their Frogeye bonnet market evaporating, Peasmarsh did not give up without a fight: in February 1962 they introduced a different hardtop for the Spridget which they fervently hoped would catch on. It was of decidedly rounded shape, rather like the original, but with a notchback window inspired by

MG versions of the Spridget had their interior matting moulded thicker and to a different pattern; their seats also looked far plusher. You could also tell them apart from a Sprite by their white, rather than black, steering wheels—distinctly Hollywood! Extra badges and a more distinctive grain on the dashboard covering were also the preserve of MG owners who could afford to part with ten quid more. Oddly enough, they also got the same instruments, but they had more distinctive markings, which were easier to read. The interior mirror remained on the scuttle top on all models.

Ford's very popular new 105E Anglia. It may not have appealed to everybody, but the idea was sound—to keep the rear screeen clean—and it did have a double skin for better insulation.

Just over a year after their introduction, the Spridgets were updated in October 1962 with a 1,098-cc engine and baulk ring synchromesh as part of sweeping changes to bring BMC's small cars into line.

The increase in engine capacity was not achieved easily. Most of the development work took place in the top-selling line, the Mini, with its transverse power train installation. In this case, the A-series engine had to have a longer crankshaft so that a primary gear and the clutch could be accommodated between the rear main bearing and the flywheel. This lowered the crankshaft's torsional vibration frequency from 29,400 to 24,300 cycles per minute. Fortunately the fourth order period of resonance, which is the real killer for a four-cylinder crankshaft, remained outside the running range up to 6,000 rpm, and higher order resonances at lower speeds had amplitudes too small to be dangerous. But the longer-stroke Morris 1100 engine which came next—and upon which the new Sprite engine was based—had to be fitted with torsional vibration dampers to prevent rapid wear and the timing gear shattering. A basic weakness here emerged in that the main bearings were only 1.875 inches in diameter although the new crankshaft had thicker webs and narrower journals.

There were also problems in that the bore had to be increased to 64.58 mm, which left less than 0.375 ins of metal between the siamesed cylinders. Even then a stroke of 83.72 mm was needed, which left insufficient room for a clamped little end. The fully floating pin which replaced it made production more complicated in that pins had to be sorted into three grade sizes to suit the production tolerances of the piston bosses and little-end bushes. Using the same 8.3:1 compression ratio cylinder head as the recently-introduced MG 1100 saloon, the Spridgets were now endowed with 55 bhp at 5,500 rpm, with 61 lb/ft

Period accessories frequently fitted to the early Spridgets included badge bars, and in this case, a device known as an Icelert, to warn of freezing road conditions.

The half-elliptic rear spring Spridgets introduced in 1964 also had a far more attractive interior with wind-up windows, quarter lights and proper exterior door handles. Items such as the luggage boot handle were improved with a more conventional horizontal double-finger grip but the pressed wheel ventilation holes were abandoned, large slots proving adequate.

The Sprite version carried on with a chrome mesh grille, but no alcohol this time, although it had a plentiful supply of Swiss misses!

of torque at an even lower speed, 2,500 rpm. The crankcase casting was also changed to one of a ribbed pattern to reduce rumble.

The synchromesh in the gearbox was much improved in that it was now the baulks ring type. Compared with the old constant load synchromesh, it gave lighter, more crashproof, changes—but there was still no synchronisation on first gear, because BMC did not consider that the saloons needed it. The power train as a whole was strengthened by the use of a double thickness gearbox plate, and the clutch diameter was raised to 7.25 ins to cope with the extra torque— which pleased tuners no end!

Disc brakes were on their way in on the BMC range, so the Spridgets got them, too. But to the Healeys' chagrin, they had to be Lockheed units rather than the Girling disc brakes they had been supplying as extras and fitting to works cars. They naturally felt an allegiance to Girlings, which had been developed from the Dunlop discs they used at an early point on their larger 100S cars. But BMC had an agreement that all cars with A-series units had to use Lockheed brakes and those with B-series power, such as the MGB, had Girlings. It didn't matter much to the public, because Lockheeds were perfectly good brakes—or would have been had the design of the front suspension allowed the use of sufficiently large discs. But as it was, they were confined to 8.25 ins which meant that relatively fast-wearing pads had to be used as the corporate purse would not stretch to fitting a servo as standard. Hence the brake pads of early Spridgets wore out very quickly and could have a tendency to fade unless harder linings, and a servo to cope with the higher pedal pressures needed, were fitted. Later, however, manufacturers developed better linings, so this problem does not exist today.

Carpets everywhere, a redesigned dashboard, parcel shelf and three-spoke steering wheel made the Sprite much more inviting inside. Spridgets also received much thicker seats and proper door trim at last, which had the unfortunate effect of reducing interior space for the occupants. Never mind, it had a much better mirror now, like that of the MGB, which could be adjusted over a far wider range up and down its new mounting rod ... and, wait for it, little slots in between the rev counter and speedometer so that the old indicator light didn't have to be covered with masking tape to avoid that blinking dazzle.

The hood was also a neat fit on the new slightly-rounded windscreen, which had securing clips at the back of its top rail.

The 1275-cc Spridgets looked much the same as before, but they had a permanently-attached hood which was much quicker to raise when it rained ... and the hub cap logos were restored! Young bucks now tried promoting their wares in a park rather than from a pub bench.

It was hardly surprising that the interior fittings of the Spridgets were brought more into line at this point. The Sprites acquired MG-style furnishings and both cars got carpets—and the MG-built hardtop became the standard option.

It was 18 months before the engine was put right with 2 inch main bearings to eliminate those awful vibrations, which had manifested themselves in distinctly rough running at high revs. Power was increased to 59 bhp at 5,750 rpm, chiefly by the old dodge of raising the compression ratio to 9:1, although the manifolds were revised at the same time. The exhaust did away with a power-sapping double bend in the down pipe. Better breathing was promoted by larger inlet valves—of 1.219 ins—and a general reshaping of the siamesed inlet tracts to reduce the 'uvula' between the ports.

A new works hardtop was designed with rear quarter lights for better visibility and concealed attachment points on the windscreen.

When the bumpers were redesigned along British Leyland corporate lines in 1969, the chrome blanking plates disappeared at last ... space was also left for a vertical number plate in view of the fact that the majority of Spridgets went to America.

Matt black sills, with a bright divider, replaced the old colour ones, although the pressing remained the same. Individual models were denoted by their name in badge form on the front of the sills, the idea being to make both Austin Healeys and MGs simply Leylands.

There were two other far-reaching changes in the new cars for the London Motor Show in October 1964: the adoption of Enever's half-elliptic rear suspension, and a redesigned interior with wind-up windows to combat the Triumph Spitfire menace, plus the option—at last—of wire wheels to give a sportier appearance.

Enever had taken particular pains to reduce unsprung weight when redesigning the rear suspension. It was a bonus that almost balanced out the penalty of the interior changes. That the new Spridgets weighed only 6 lb more overall was due to the sort of cheeseparing work that comes only with extensive experience and development. For a start, the new half elliptic springs were about one third of the weight of the quarter elliptics, because they had only five, thinner, leaves; this also made them a lot more supple. It was possible to eliminate the parallelogram radius arms, brackets and mountings and much of the localised stiffening around the front mounts. The new springs were held firmly in a new front mount with a rear shackle pivoting on a bracket to accommodate deflections. Lever arm shock absorbers had to be retained to save money, with the right-hand one having a new SU electric fuel pump mounted above it. This was all part of a corporate policy to eliminate the earlier engine-driven fuel pump, but suffered from having to be placed in a position where it was exposed to a great deal of road debris. It was all very well in theory, being sited in the best place to suck the last drop of petrol out of the tank, but in practice it would have been better to have fitted it to a cleaner and more accessible area, such as the scuttle.

The new interior was a dramatic improvement in many ways. The wind-up windows were curved slightly to allow more elbow room, which had been encroached upon by their occupation of what had been the door pockets. Quarter lights were fitted not only to give an extra variation for ventilation, but to provide a vertical guide for the front of the windows. The space below the quarter lights inside the doors was occupied by the bulk of the window-winding mechanism. Neatly recessed anti-burst interior door handles linked to lockable outer handles were a vast improvement—even if they were mounted in an infernally difficult position to reach! In keeping with modern trends, the windscreen was curved slightly for better overall aerodynamics, although it was now noticeable that the slipstream whipped round the back of the occupants' necks. The new screen also necessitated a tie rod being fitted in the centre to hold its top rail firmly in place. This adaptation of MGB practice allowed the interior mirror to be clamped on it at any height that suited the driver; a considerable improvement on the former scuttle-mounted mirror which caused a blind spot for forward vision. The loss of the door pockets was partly compensated for by a rather floppy crushable parcel shelf on the passenger's side. At the same time, the instrument panel was revised with a binnacle in front of the driver, in which the rev counter and speedometer were angled to fall in the ideal plane for the eyes' focus. A new 17-inch steering wheel, with its three spokes angled for maximum vision, helped ... and it also had a modern indicator stalk on its column at last. The quality of the carpets and trim was

Last of the Sprites ... with an Austin badge on its matt-black grille.

improved and although the seats were made to feel more comfortable, the overall result was a slight infringement on cockpit space.

The next major changes were two years later, in October 1966, when the Spridget's engine capacity went up to 1,275 cc and a much more sophisticated hood was adopted. The cylinder block and 10-stud head were the same as those used on the most potent Mini Cooper S, with a bore and stroke of 70.6 mm × 80.3. But the power output was restricted to 64 bhp at 5,600 (with 72 lb/ft or torque at 3,000 rpm) rather than 76 bhp, so that cheaper materials could be used. At first, BMC thought they could get away with using their normal forged crankshaft, but this showed signs of strain on early engines, so they hurriedly substituted the expensive Cooper S nitrided steel crank, until it became apparent that a cheaper Tuftrided shaft was enough to cope with 64 bhp. Although the Cooper S head was used, cheaper Mini Cooper valves were fitted, with dished pistons to reduce the 9.7:1 compression ratio to a more restrained 8.7:1.

A new diaphragm clutch was introduced to give lighter and smoother operation without any loss of bite. It was still operated hydraulically, but separate master cylinders were now used for the brakes and clutch. These were in anticipation of dual circuit braking being demanded by American legislation. An almost unheralded change was the substitution of roller bearings in the gearbox to replace bronze bushes, which were rather weak.

The new hood was a much more modern affair which would have gained the Spridget the designation drop-head coupé had it been introduced in 1958! Because its material and frame was permanently attached to the rear part of the cockpit, it was a lot quicker to raise in the event of a sudden storm. Lowering was easier, too, and the hood could be stowed beneath a neat cover in settled weather. It was at this point that the retention of the lever arm shock absorbers really came into its own. In later days, when virtually all cars had vertical, or near-vertical, telescopic dampers, the towers needed to locate them often prevented a hood being packed within the car's rear deck. In many cases, when the hood was down on such cars, it was not really down at all, but stacked halfway up in the air rather like an old-fashioned cabriolet. However, the Spridgets looked as good as ever with their new hoods down.

Early in 1968, the electrical system was converted from positive earth to negative earth so that an alternator could be fitted, but this improved, and more expensive, form of generator would be a long time coming! Later that year, a

The squared-off rear wheel opening saw out the Sprite, fitted here with the attractive cast alloy wheels as standard.

Luggage racks continued to be popular fittings that could be removed, leaving only their mounting plates, when they were not needed.

3.9:1 final drive ratio replaced the 4.2 (with an attendant change in speedometer gearing), for improved fuel economy and more relaxed high-speed cruising.

The changes that followed were often more political than practical. Matt black paint reared its ugly head all over the cars in October 1969. Not only did they have the same price for the first time, but the Spridgets received identical recessed grilles, black sills and a sombre new windscreen frame. The standard wheels, also in matt black, looked a lot better, however: they were cast rather than pressed. The bumpers were remodelled on BL's corporate slim-line theme, with the rear blade being divided to make way for a vertical number plate in the middle. It was rather belated recognition of what the Americans needed! The exhaust system was revised to incorporate two silencers, one running across the back, because of European noise regulations. Leyland badges also made their appearance as part of BL's new policy to ease out marque names, although the old Austin Healey and MG badges were retained for the time being, but in much smaller form. The actual model names, Sprite and Midget, were emphasised in chrome on the matt black sills, the austere competition-oriented nature of which was relieved by long chrome strips! But the Spridget was no longer badged as a Sprite for North America because British Leyland decided to drop the Austin Healey name there, pointing out that far more Midgets had been sold since 1961, for nostalgic reasons. Thankfully, they were able to drop

Front view of the last of the chrome-bumper Midgets, still giving its driver a good time in 1983, ten years after it left Abingdon.

the ugly black windscreen surround soon after its introduction and revert to its normal aluminium finish because anticipated American legislation on the matter was forthcoming.

But new American laws that did come into force meant that the interior had to be revised again with rocker switches, safety handles and a collapsible steering column. Reclining seats with a wider range of adjustment were offered at the same time.

A year later, the Austin Healey name was dropped altogether and for a few months, until June 1971, Spridgets were called either Austins or MGs. But it was at this time, early in 1970, that 10 years' hard pleading by customers at last won an automatic stay to keep the boot lid open when their arms were full of shopping. They also got a light for the boot, and, glory be, one for the interior. The bonnet got an automatic stay, too. But what a pity the cast wheels were replaced with pressed steel imitation ones by Rostyle. The fuel tank was made a little bigger, at seven gallons, and a steering column lock fitted. But by June 1971, the name Sprite had been dropped and all Spridgets became Midgets.

Radial-ply tyres, which had long been available as options, were fitted as standard in January 1972, and for some reason which remains a mystery, the rear wheel arches were rounded, rather than squared-off. Possibly it made the wheels easier to change, but it certainly weakened the wings to impacts from the rear. The money spent on this retooling might have been better spent on the front wings, because the front suspension was raised half an inch to meet new American legislation on headlamp heights. But the alternator arrived at last ...

More detail changes followed in the next year, with hazard warning lights having been made compulsory, before, at last, the front anti-roll bar that the Healeys had been campaigning for since the Spridget was in its prototype stage was fitted as standard!

IV

The Rubber-Bumpered Spridgets

Eventually there were no more detail changes that could be made to cope with snowballing American environmental regulations. The Midget had to be completely revised, rather than slightly altered by just hanging on more anti-emission equipment and changing switches, door handles and other small items. There was no way it could meet laws that now meant that it had to survive being rammed into a concrete block at 5 mph with all legal necessities intact. In addition, it had to have bumpers set at a certain height—that of the average large American saloon. These regulations were probably framed as the result of politicians' experiences in supermarket parking lots. They had nothing to do with reality on the road, where, in end-to-end accidents, almost invariably the car about to crash into another one's tail had its brakes applied, even if only at the last moment. This depressed the nose with the result that if all bumpers were at the same height, the front bumper went under that of the car in front. At the same time, the rear bumper of the crashing car went up, well above the height of anything following with regulation bumpers. The only these bumpers were of any real use was when cars were being used like dodgems in a parking spot. It was no small wonder that insurance claims soared as they wreaked havoc with bodywork, such was their strength. Nevertheless, the Midget had to meet these bumper regulations if it was to be sold in its biggest market, the United States. British Leyland's development was based on that for the soon-to-be-announced Triumph TR7.

Both front and rear bumpers were produced with an energy-absorbing moulding of urethene foam surrounding a massive steel bar, and a black polycarbonate cover at the front and a nylon one at the back to withstand the ravishes of sloppy fuel fillers. Although these bumpers were not made of rubber, they looked as though they were and had some measure of flexibility, so the cars that resulted were christened 'rubber-bumpered Spridgets.'

Needless to say, there was more than met the eye about fitting such massive bumpers and making the structure strong enough to withstand the protection they afforded. Massive reinforcement had to be made to the front and the back areas of the existing floorpan, which was retained to keep the cost within reasonable bounds. The front and rear aprons also had to be restyled to fit neatly

The Midget was altered as little as possible when it was fitted with the massive new American-style bumpers, but the ride height had to be raised, more because of their extra weight than from having to meet a minimum height. In the circumstances, with very little capital available after a fortune had been spent on development to meet emission restrictions, the new bumpers moulded in quite well with the existing lines. They have also proved extraordinarily effective in coping with city parking problems! Rostyle pressed steel wheels of a pattern that became popular in the 1970s were fitted as standard at the same time.

The new Triumph 1500 power unit undergoing development in a Midget engine bay. Everything had to be swopped around, giving some accessibility problems and difficulty with the exhaust system.

around the bumpers, which had to be mounted higher than before. The total weight of all this work was around 200 lb, which, by rule of thumb, could be regarded as a 100 lb weight on either end of the pendulum formed by the floorpan. As a result, it was no good mounting the bumper beams at the regulation height and leaving the Midget's ground clearance unaltered. The ride height had to be raised by 1 inch or the suspension would have had to have been stiffened to an unacceptable degree to stop the car bottoming. This rise was achieved by changing the front cross-member mounting and recambering the rear springs with six leaves instead of five. Ironically, the rear wheel arches had to be squared-off again to provide sufficient strength at the back. The extra weight had one advantage that might have been overlooked: it improved the Midget's ride. But with steering alterations, it changed the handling once and for all. The car rolled a lot more now, although the anti-roll bar, which had just been standardised, did a lot to limit the movement. The chief dimension affected by such 'progress' was the length: it went up by just over 3.5 ins to 11 ft 9 ins.

With so much extra weight to haul around, the Midget needed more power if its performance was to remain anything near like so good as before. This was particularly apparent with the strangulated American versions, which even had to have an additional exhaust restriction in the biggest individual market, California. In company with the softer appeal of the car—the ride and a lower-ratio steering rack being the most noticeable aspects—it needed more torque, too. This meant that the engine had to go up in capacity, and the aged A-series unit was at the limit of its practical development in this sphere. The Spitfire was

Attention was paid to giving the interior a better quality appeal with leather edging for the carpets, a leather gearlever boot, and reclining seats. The steering wheel rim was trimmed in leather in a style which had been pioneered by racing and grand touring cars. Safety-conscious rocker switches and less-prominent window winders and quarter light levers replaced the earlier hard-edged plastic knobs and chrome fittings.

Late-style US Midgets in production at Abingdon with safety hub nuts on their optional wire wheels.

suffering from the same basic problems, so the solution was obvious: now the two rivals were in the same British Leyland camp, the Midget would be fitted with the Spitfire's engine, which, it just so happened, could be expanded enough to give it a lot more torque.

This engine was Triumph's equivalent of the A-series. It had similar overall dimensions and weighed about the same—which was hardly surprising as it was of the same four-cylinder configuration and had started life in the same capacity, 803 cc, to power Standard's equivalent of the A30, the Eight, in 1953. Like the A-series unit, which it resembled in all but a few details, it had been stretched to 1,296 cc for the Mark III Spitfire, among other cars. The chief differences were that its oil pump (and distributor) drive was taken from the middle of the camshaft and the pushrod tubing passed the sparking plugs. A great deal of siamesing had gone on as its capacity expanded and there was now no room for a bigger bore. For production economy, the machined depth between the top and bottom cylinder faces had to remain the same as well. But the big difference between the former rivals was that Triumph had managed to change the throw of their crankshaft so much that a considerably longer stroke raised the capacity to 1,493 cc for the 1500 saloon in 1970. Its eventual dimensions were a bore and stroke of 73.7 mm × 87.5 mm—rather long, but good enough. A six-cylinder development in the Triumph TR5 had an even longer-throw crankshaft, which in four-cylinder form, would have given the engine 1,621 cc. So British Leyland were happy in the knowledge that they could stretch it even further, if need be.

This engine had already been used in the 1973 Spitfires sold on the American market, producing 57 bhp at 5,000 rpm with full emission equipment, and 71 lb/ft or torque at 3,000 rpm, the sort of power that the A-series had in this market. So this was the engine that went into the US rubber-bumper Midgets with a single Zenith-Stromberg carburettor and a compression ratio of 7.5:1. In its British form, with twin 1.5-inch SUs and a 9:1 compression ratio,

Rostyle wheels proved more popular on British Midgets although wire wheels still had their fans.

Hood up, the 'rubber-bumper' Midget is still as snug as ever and not so much different in concept from that of the first Frogeye.

the Spitfire's 1,500 cc engine produced 71 bhp and 82 lb/ft of torque, but it had to have a different exhaust system for installation in a Midget. Unfortunately, this cut the power to 65 bhp. It was the same as that quoted for the 1,275 cc A-series unit, but it was really a bit higher because BL's power outputs were now quoted to tighter standards. But whichever way you looked at it, the torque was up, by 4.5 lb/ft to 76.5, and this made all the difference.

It meant that a wider-ratio all-synchromesh gearbox from the 1.3-litre Morris Marina saloon could be used, although a closer-ratio version was also available from the 1.8-litre Marina. When the new gearbox's lower ratios of, first, 3.41, second, 2.11, third, 1.43, and a direct top (reverse was 3.75:1) were combined with the existing 3.9:1 final drive, the extra pulling power easily overcame the higher weight. A better top speed also resulted, partly due to improved aerodynamics and partly to more honest horsepower.

Other changes included fitting the Spitfire's lower-geared steering—to give 2.75 turns from lock to lock rather than 2.25—now that the Marina had replaced the Minor. New track control arms were also needed. The Midget had changed its character so much at this point that few people complained.

Numerous other minor alterations were made as the Midget continued to sell well in this form with little to rival it at first, apart from the Spitfire. Headrests were fitted as standard from January 1977, with inertia reel seatbelts three months later. The cooling system had to be improved at the same time as ever-tightening emission regulations resulted in engines running hotter on leaner fuel. This problem was made worse by the reduced size of the air intake in the rubber-bumpered front. The rear axle ratio was raised to 3.72:1 to keep revs in check and the car in line with other BL products, in September 1977. Midgets sprouted a door mirror at the same time to keep within EEC regulations, and the instruments were revised to use those of the MGB for America and the same as the Spitfire elsewhere. This meant that the European Midgets lost their octagonal cockpit badge.

It remained only for duel circuit brakes to be fitted at last in October 1978 before the last Spridget left the lines in November.

V

Contemporary Road Testers' Reports

It is small wonder that the Sprite got off to such a magnificent start. Early road tests served only to emphasise its mouth-watering appeal. They explained how potential owners would soon get used to steering which would seem very twitchy at first and treated such features as the dark hole where luggage could be stored with a brand of good humour that was to stick with the model for life. In fact there was hardly any criticism ... just a great deal of welcoming applause.

Thanks to a three-week stint with one of the prototypes, registered PBL 75, before the official launch, *The Motor* became the first specialist magazine to publish a road test of the Sprite in their issue of 21 May 1958. This set the seal on all the tests to follow by pointing out that the pert newcomer presented an amazing pleasure-to-price ratio. 'Costing about as much to buy as do many popular saloons of similar one-litre engine size, and perhaps even cheaper than such saloons to run, this open two-seater offers much better acceleration up to a top speed which is higher by some 10 mph, but responsiveness to the slightest touch on the controls is what really makes it such a joy to drive,' said *The Motor's* scribes. They added of the steering:

> 'With no evident lost motion whatever, seemingly negligible friction, and quite light self-centring effect, this steering lets the car be guided by use of fingers and wrists rather than by arm movements—the near-vertical two-spoke wheel is set too close to the seat to permit the straight-arm driving position which is fashionable with racing drivers of cars with lower-geared steering. Naturally enough, this is a car which corners fast with little or no roll, squealing its tyres only under very severe provocation, and in a corner it shows a modest degree of stable "understeer" until the limit of tyre adhesion is reached. Perhaps because the natural sensitivity of the steering is magnified by flexible rubber bushes in some of the front and rear suspension pivots, the car needs a decidedly delicate touch on the controls to put it into a corner fast and accurately on a chosen line without initial "oversteering" by the driver, and too heavy a hand on the controls will accentuate a slight tendency to weave on the straight at maximum speeds. Once a sensitive driver has the feel of this car, however, he can revel in hustling it along winding roads, totally forgetting a tendency for the car to

pull slightly to the right during acceleration or left on the overrun which at first acquaintance was fairly evident. Wet and slippery roads do nothing to diminish the pleasure of driving this light and outstandingly responsive car, and rough roads do not jolt it unduly despite the suspension being much firmer than on most modern touring cars.'

Sports car folk were used to a far rougher ride in those days! The days were not long gone, either when they could carry only a limited amoung of luggage on exposed racks, so *The Motor* felt constrained only to say:

'Accommodation for a considerable volume of luggage is available behind the seats, in a long and reasonably wide compartment of reasonable height. But this space can be reached only from the front past tilted-forward seat backrests, and small items can become lost in its depths.'

The steering gear that set the Sprite on its sucessful path ... 'with no evident lost motion whatever, seemingly negligible friction and quite light self-centring effect,' said *The Motor*.

The dashboard and gearlever with which Mr Meisl of *Sports Cars Illustrated* had painful memories after testing the Frogeye.

The performance figures of an 83-mph maximum speed, 20.5-second 0–60 mph time, 21.8-second standing quarter mile, and fuel consumption between 33 mpg and 43 mpg when treated more gently, were comfortably superior to all but the largest saloons and quite competitive with other sports cars in those days.

One of *The Motor's* rival weekles, *Autosport*, was able to publish driving impressions by technical editor John Bolster on 23 May 1958, because he had been involved three months earlier in a promotional film on the Sprite with racing driver Roy Salvadori, retained to publicise Austin Healeys. Bolster reported:

'I was able to test the car at Silverstone under all conditions from fairly dry to atrociously wet. It was also allowed to take it on the road, although the furore it created in a public house car park was a little embarrassing ...

The Autocar were appreciative of the hardtop on their Sprite, although it led to a considerable increase in noise. The car in the picture is the Sprite used by Pat Moss and Ann Wisdom to finish second in class in the 1960 RAC Rally.

'My first impression concerned the remarkable quietness of the Sprite. Even with the hood up, one could converse in a normal tone of voice, and I am so glad that the tradition of noisy sports cars is at last on the wane.

'As I expected, the four-speed gearbox proved ideal for fast driving. Third speed is high enough for fast corners or overtaking and second is a useful traffic gear. The short, central, lever is nicely placed, and in fact the driving position is first class. The steering is quicker than that of most production cars, in the interests of rapid skid correction. One perhaps tends to oversteer the car at first for this reason, particularly on a narrow, bumpy, road. However the effect soon wears off with practice.

'The roadholding is good, and the general controllability on wet roads is excellent. The behaviour of the rear axle is far better under these conditions than that of a conventional semi-elliptic rear end.'

With those rather controversial assertions, Bolster added that the brakes were well able to cope with the light weight.

The Autocar continued in similar euphoric vein when they tested PBL 75, echoing the comments of their fellow weeklies on 20 June 1958. They obviously enjoyed their tenure with the Sprite very much, particularly because it could be handled with such agility. They reported:

'A clear indication of the superiority of the Sprite is this respect over most family cars—and several sports cars, too—is provided when the little car is on the tail of one of them on a twisty road. During the test this occurred several times, and even while the car ahead was being driven near the limit of its adhesion, the Sprite remained as unruffled as a sphinx.'

Nobody ever likened a Sprite to a sphinx again, but *The Autocar* were less impassive when it came to the gearbox. They said second gear was too low and backed up their argument with statistics: 'The maximum speeds on the three

The hardtop on John Sprinzel's personal Sprite, PMO 200, came complete with a new screen and surround, which was grafted on to the scuttle at a line where the leading edge of the door was angled away to its top rail.

Alexander marketed similar modified equipment to that of Speedwell for Sprites, with their demonstrator, registered 777 EBH, featuring a slightly different hardtop, with a larger rear window, that was bolted to the scuttle along a normal line, and a bonnet with more rounded wings.

One of the Healey Motor Company's most popular lines was a large wood-rimmed steering wheel with a Sprite-type motif in the middle.

indirects are 23, 37 and 63 mph. The gap between the second and third gear maximum is therefore 26, while between first and second it is only 14.' But then they mollified their criticism by saying:

'A slightly higher first and adoption of an appreciably higher second would be welcome, although it is realised that the present choice, which results from the use of standard BMC parts, helps to keep down the price.'

The Autocar had a valid criticism over the gearchange as well; pointing out that:

'A stronger safety spring against reverse would make a small improvement. On the car tested the change across the narrow gate from second to third

The Healey works car that was to race at Le Mans with a special body in 1960 featured disc brakes at the front and an anti-roll bar, which can be seen at the bottom left of the picture, with its mounting bracket bolted to the lower suspension arm.

could be affected by catching the opening to the reverse slot; and when changing from third to top as quickly as possible it was necessary to avoid using much pressure to hold the lever to the right, for fear of touching reverse itself. These criticisms appear more serious on paper than they proved to be in practice; they did not slow accurately-executed changes.'

And their comments on the cockpit and luggage compartment showed how much they appreciated a car that was obviously a bargain:

'The luggage boot's shortcomings are accounted for by the competitive price and the extra rigidity provided by the one-piece, non-opening rear end. Stowage and removal of luggage and the spare wheel are not ideally simple, and oddments, once let loose in the cavity, are difficult to retrieve. However, with the use of soft bags the total volume of luggage which can be carried is greater than one would expect in a sports car of this size. There is a space between the seats and the luggage compartment proper which can take casual accoutrements, and even a young child (owing not so much to the shape as the childish liking for wriggling into unpromising crannies).'

Performance figures were largely similar to those recorded by *The Motor*, although the fact that the exhaust pipe snapped and the top speed was lower at 80 mph might have been some indication of the hard life that PBL 75 was leading. Charles Meisl gave credence to this theory in the first road test with the car for a specialist monthly. He wrote in the British edition of *Sports Cars Illustrated* in August 1958:

'Any over-enthusiastic cornering is checked with the flick of the wrist. We purposely induced four-wheel "driftlets" during the prevailing damp weather and the Sprite behaved like a full-grown racing machine, being controllable to an inch. Poor roads set up a slight fore and aft pitch, especially at slowish speeds, this also produces sundry rattles and squeaks.

The Healey hardtop was secured by exposed clips to the top of the windscreen surround.

Some of the rattles on the test car were traced to the choke and throttle cables drumming against the bonnet, and in fairness it must be said that the test car had had a tough life! The squeak seemed to come from one of the rubber bushes of the rear torque arms or perhaps from excessive dryness of one of the rear quarter elliptic springs ... '

Then Mr Meisl added with feeling:

'I disliked the length of the gearlever. It is too easy to bark one's knuckles (I did twice) on the lower edge of the fascia in bottom and third gear positions ... The interior bent tin door handles are placed so that an energetic manoeuvre brings them into violent and painful contact with the driver's elbow, they are unworthy of such a delightful little car ...

'Accessibility to the engine and front suspension is good, although when closed the bonnet tends to flutter up and down a little at speed. Stronger hinges might obviate this trouble. Improvement of the bonnet lock would also be desirable; again it is likely to trap unwary fingers and knuckles. The horn sounds like a hysterical canary.'

Nevertheless, the general tenure of his report was not only what a bargain the Sprite offered, but what a charming car it was with it's 'cheerful smiling countenance.' His colleagues on the American edition of *Sports Cars Illustrated* felt much the same and were more voluble in their edition on August 1958. They said:

'BMC has changed the spelling of the word fun. It's now a six-letter word: Sprite. It even looks happy ...

'On first look you feel as though you would like to pat it on the head—if it had one to pat. Virtually everybody who has driven it has much the same reactions. First the feeling described above, then a sort of "cute car, but will it go?" feeling. One block of driving and nobody cars how fast it is. The pure enjoyment of handling this willing little box is such that true performance doesn't matter very much—you're having too much of a ball to dither about trifles. It pounces around in traffic like a playful kitten, goes when it's told and stops when bidden. Its steering is the sort of thing automobile writers dream about and seldom experience, even on pure-bred racing machinery. Light withal, it gives a feeling of utter reliability ... Sprites are ideal first sports cars for either the beginner in The True Motoring whose tastes formerly leaned towards the titanic, or the novice to sports racing who wants to feel his way around the race course.'

They then proceded to do just that, trying the Sprite at Lime Rock in the manner that so many of the people who bought these cars were to do in the early years. It came through these tests with flying colours—every member of the staff of *Sports Cars Illustrated* tried the Sprite—although their comments on the ride were amusing:

'The axle is ... equipped with a strap that over a spring-busting bump will transfer some of the impact overload on the shocks to the base of the spine. Shocks on both ends, incidentally, are non-tubular and smack very strongly of our own GM practice in the 40s ... Despite the short wheelbase the Sprite rides extremely well over choppy roads and aside from a tendency to scrape the number plate on either end (shades of the Austin Healey 100-Six!), handles the dipsy doodles very well.'

The writer then went on to describe how it had been impossible to squeeze his weekend suitcase into the Big Healey's trunk, but how the said suitcase proved to be ideal in conjunction with the Sprite's 'cavernous' luggage compartment. It was just the spare wheel that was worrisome.

'Our prayers protecting us against flats were answered, as it is necessary to crawl into the cramped rearward recesses to remove the spare. After the first such mishap, BMC would have no trouble marketing, as an optional extra, a trained monkey to load and unload the spare and the tools.'

Performance figures were well up to European standards with those of the rival American magazine, *Road & Track*, in the same month, slightly slower with a 78.5-mph maximum because they used only 5,500 rpm in deference to a tight-feeling engine. *Road & Track* were also the first publication to compare the headlights with the eyes of a frog, although doubtless the thought had crossed many minds before. They pointed out that second gear was much too low, except, significantly—'for those drivers who like to use the American three-

The Shorrock supercharger was bolted on the left of the engine when viewed from the front, replacing the normal inlet manifold. Its drive was taken from the front of the crankshaft by twin belts, with a single 2-inch SU carburetter fitted to the back of the new manifold.

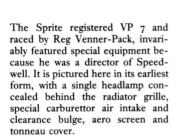

The Sprite registered VP 7 and raced by Reg Venner-Pack, invariably featured special equipment because he was a director of Speedwell. It is pictured here in its earliest form, with a single headlamp concealed behind the radiator grille, special carburettor air intake and clearance bulge, aero screen and tonneau cover.

speeds forward pattern'—and pleaded for a higher rear axle ratio of about 3.9:1 to make 70 mph cruising less fussy. 'Of course 5,000 rpm and 76 mph is theoretically safe, but the engine is spinning a little too fast at that rate to feel really serene for hours at a time ... ' Those were the days in the Land of the Free ...

The British monthly, *Motor Sport*, agreed with their contemporaries when it came in September 1958 to describing how their Sprite, registered WON 667, handled and performed, with the addition of some far-reaching comments. They said:

> 'The screen is fixed and we dislike the sharp-edged flanges that take the sidescreens; anyone unlucky enough to let his Sprite tumble over might be badly hurt by these if the screen collapsed.
>
> 'To gain access to the engine compartment, the whole bonnet, inclusive of headlamps, hinges up and is automatically propped open, after a toggle lever has been turned and a safety catch released. The bonnet is very heavy, making this no light task. It could be fatal were the stay to collapse with the owner "under the lid," while shutting the bonnet provokes the response "*******!" as one's hand is trapped between the bonnet and front number plate. After this one tended to drop the lid, but a sidelamp, secured only by its rubber flange, fell into the road ... these are trifling criticisms balanced against the fun of getting into the Sprite and motoring it about.'

By the time *The Autocar* tested a Sprite, registered YOE 312, with a glass fibre hardtop marketed by the Donald Healey Motor Company, on 20 November 1959, the model had become well established. They said of the £50 hardtop:

> 'A first-class fit results with the hardtop in position, and draughts are eliminated almost completely. There is no leakage in heavy rain, but a

considerable noise increase is noticed at speed, in comparison with the open or hood-up conditions. Exhaust boom and wind road combine to make the car decidedly noisy at more than 60 mph which, although for-giveable on a sports car, will perhaps be unwelcome to the class of motorist who will specify the hardtop for protection against the elements ...

'In relation to the Sprite tested last year, the acceleration is comparable, and shows a slight gain at the higher speeds. This suggests that the hardtop shape offers less wind resistance than the hood—borne out by a 5 mph increase in the best top gear maximum speed.'

In this form, *The Autocar* recorded an 84.1-mph top speed (with an 86-mph best one-way run) with a 0–60 mph time of 23.7 seconds, and 0–70 of 33.4 seconds and standing quarter mile in 33.4 seconds. And in many future cases, Sprites modified for higher performance were to be fitted with hardtops.

Modified Frogeyes

The tuning industry in Britain was moving into full swing when the first Sprites appeared, with John Bolster having the opportunity to try a Speedwell Sprite at a very early point. This car was standard except that it was fitted with an engine of the type used in the Austin A35 for saloon car racing. This featured a gas-flowed head, 1.25 inch SU carburettors and special manifolds. During this test reported in *Autosport* on 20 June 1958, Bolster recorded a top speed of 91.8 mph with improved acceleration times of 19.4 seconds for the 0–60 and 19.8 seconds for the standing quarter mile. These figures were taken in very wet conditions, however, and he felt that they could have been better with less wheelspin.

By the time Douglas Armstrong tested the same car—the first demon-strator built by Speedwell—for the August 1958 issue of *Sports Cars Illustrated*'s British edition, it was looking very travel-stained, but still going well. With 15 stone of Armstrong aboard, plus a similar-sized passenger, the car certainly did not suffer from wheelspin! But despite the best part of 4 cwt of passengers and equipment, it did the 0–60 in 20 seconds and achieved 88 mph flat out with the hood down, with obvious potential for more in an improved aerodynamic state with the hood up. This car, the first Sprite to bear the registration number PMO 200, had also been fitted with a front anti-roll bar by the time Armstrong tried it, which evoked favourable comment.

The Speedwell Sprite had an 8.7:1 compression ratio head for 'more than 50 bhp', whereas their chief rivals, Alexander, had fitted a higher, 9.4:1, head to their Sprite for *Motor Racing*'s test in January 1959. It also had a fully balanced bottom end and cold air box for the carburettors, otherwise the engine modifications were similar to those made by Speedwell. But it seemed to have produced only about the same power as the Speedwell car, with a 19.6-second standing quarter mile and 89-mph top speed with full weather equipment. Overall fuel consumption was around 10 per cent higher at 29 mpg. David Phipps also tried this car registered 777 EBH, in the trim normally used for racing, with a small plastic aero screen that dramatically reduced the frontal area. The results were startling: a 98-mph top speed with 100 mph being achieved on one of the two opposite-direction runs. Acceleration was around 10 per cent better than with the full-sized screen in place. Suspension and braking modifications amounted only to a front anti-roll bar and servo, however, and as an indication of contemporary standards, Phipps felt that this was enough.

Far more extensive modifications were made to the running gear of a Sprite prepared by Healeys at Warwick and tested by *The Motor* for the 22 April 1959, issue. This was the car, registered 5983 AC, that was later to be rebodied to race at Le Mans in 1960. In its 1959 form it featured all the tuning gear that the Donald Healey Motor Company was considering selling to enthusiastic owners wishing to uprate their cars to full-race—or rally—specification.

In fact some of the parts were very rare—being listed in *The Motor*'s test as having been discontinued. The idea was to see if sufficient demand could be whipped up to make it worth producing more. The engine had similar modifications to those marketed by Speedwell and Alexander, with a special camshaft, and distributor and dual exhaust system. The gearbox was a 'discontinued' close-ratio version with higher indirect gearing of 6.14, 9.05 and 13.67 linked to a lower 4.55:1 rear axle. These changes were only enough to give the 'works' Sprite a top speed of 91.6 mph, however, with slightly inferior acceleration to that of the rival examples because it had ½ cwt more tuning gear: wire wheels, front disc brakes and an anti-roll bar, plus a glass fibre hardtop. There is little doubt, though, that it would have been able to lap faster and that it handled better than the more mundane modified cars because of its far superior braking and better handling. The works hardtop was of particular advantage for rallying or long-distance racing in terms of occupant comfort, especially when

VP 7 was later rebodied along similar lines to the Speedwell Sprite raced here by Graham Hill in the 1959 Silverstone International Trophy GT event. Hill's car, registered VXT 523, is fitted with the earlier Speedwell bonnet and a 'bubble' hardtop modelled on the lines of the works Lotus Elite that is chasing it.

the 'aggressive and tiring' bark of the exhaust system was taken into consideration. The ride suffered from the dampers having been re-valved to improve the handling, the total effect being to give the Sprite a greater feeling of stability with slight, but consistent, understeer. Nevertheless, it was still a practical proposition for road work save only for the lack of a cooling fan, which caused the radiator to boil quickly in traffic. The cost of the modifications amounted to £166—less than 25 per cent more than the total price of the car in Britain because the extras were not subject to purchase tax if they were fitted after delivery.

Such modifications were far more akin to what was needed on the race track, however, than for high-speed touring, so Healeys also marketed the ultimate 'bolt-on goodie', a Shorrock supercharger, for about the same price as their engine modifications—£70 plus £10 for fitting. This raised the maximum power of a standard engine to 68 bhp at 5,700 rpm with 65 lb/ft of torque at 3,000 rpm. The extra power and torque did not seem to have a detrimental effect on either the engine or the transmission during the test and made the car far easier to drive because it became so flexible. In fact it appeared to be a thoroughly desirable improvement when combined with the wire wheels, disc brakes and anti-roll bar. David Phipps certainly liked the supercharged Sprite when he tested it for *Motor Racing* in December 1959. He wrote:

'By comparison with the standard car, the performance of the super-charged Sprite is on an altogether different plane, and its roadholding could hardly be faulted, except perhaps on fast ess-bends where a stiffer anti-roll bar might have helped on the change from one lock to the other. The slight roll oversteer of the standard Sprite is completely eliminated,

Paddy Gaston achieved a high reputation in racing and tuning circles as a result of his exploits in a Sprite registered RAM 35, stripped to the bare necessities before it received Ashley bodywork. It is fitted with an Alexander bonnet in this picture.

Sprinzel takes PMO 200 to a class win in the 1960 RAC Rally before handing it over to Pat Moss to race at Brands Hatch. By the time that John Bolster tested it for *Autospsort*, however, it had a standard-shaped hardtop and screen.

however, and this—with the positive rack-and-pinion steering—results in handling qualities which are almost up to sports racing standards. The modified brakes are well up to the increased performance, and the front disc/drum set-up seems ideally suited to this comparatively light car, additional advantages being the provision of moderate pedal pressure at all times and a really adequate handbrake.

'As to performance itself, the Shorrock supercharger completely transforms the car. Acceleration times through the gears are improved by more than 100 per cent in some cases, and at the same time the engine is smoother and more flexible than the standard unit. Maximum speed is increased by some 20 per cent, even with the normal hood and sidescreens fitted, and it seems certain that the smoother contours of a hardtop would make this a true 100 mph car.

'Such considerations are of far less importance, however, than the more practical aspects of the car's performance, particularly its remarkable "liveliness" in traffic. From any sort of check, the supercharged Sprite will accelerate back to a cruising speed not far short of its maximimum in an incredibly short time. Even in top gear it will go from 30–80 mph quicker than some 1½-litre sports cars. And the engine of the test car was so smooth at all speeds that I suspected it of being specially prepared and balanced, although I was assured that this was not the case ...

'The disc brake/wire wheel conversion, although dearer than the supercharger, also proved its worth not only by slowing the car abruptly whenever necessary, but also by imparting the comforting feeling that, however steep the decent, whatever the hazard, the Sprite would always be able to stop.'

Phipp's performance figures were especially significant when it was realised that they were taken on the same car, 5983 AC, as had been used in 'works' guise by *The Motor*. In this case with a standard gearbox and rear axle it was tested without its hardtop, achieving far better times, including a 10.8-second 0–60; directly comparable figures taken by the two magazines were, 0–50 11.6 seconds (8.2), 0–70 24 seconds (14.8), standing quarter mile 20.7 seconds (18.4) and 30.5 mpg (27). Obviously, with the exception of fuel consumption, a supercharged Sprite could be made to perform far better! However, 5983 AC seemed to be suffering somewhat when *Motor Sport* had a chance to try it in works hardtop form for their issue of December 1959, with signs of impending big-end trouble and clutch slip ...

Suspicious that 5983 AC might have had a 'hot' engine in it were increased by a third test of a supercharged Sprite from the Healeys by John Bolster in *Autosport* on 8 April 1960. This works hardtop car, of very standard appearance, could manage only 93.7 mph, although Bolster thought that it might have been able to touch 100 mph with a higher axle ratio than the standard 4.22. Its acceleration figures, however, were considerably inferior to those recorded by Phipps, the 0–60, for instance, taking 13.2 seconds with the same 27 mpg fuel

Sprinzel Sprites continued to be developed along the same lines as Speedwell Sprites. On this car, the hardtop has been moulded into the scuttle, and the bonnet made less fussy, with tiny sidelights let into the headlamp wells. This was the bodywork used on the 1961 Moss car.

Open and shut case ... the new Spridget luggage boot with its opening lid became an immediate success.

consumption. If Bolster's figures were not so good, the set recorded by *The Motor* on 19 August 1960, with another supercharged Sprite from Healeys were downright disappointing. The engine of their car, registered 7048 NX, could not reach 6,000 rpm even with a following wind, whereas previous units had gone well past this—particularly competition ones where change-up points of 6,500 were common at that time. In this form, 7048 NX was capable of only 87 mph with a 0–60 time of 15.3 seconds, so obviously supercharged Sprites varied wildly in performance despite the same power and torque figures being quoted. A clue to this car's relatively poor performance could be gleaned from the fact that it had done 14,000 miles, and probably hard ones because the gearbox's synchromesh was also suffering.

Meanwhile, tuners everywhere were trying their hand on Sprites, generally along lines adopted by Speedwell and Alexander. In the case of the Joe Virag-tuned example tested by the US edition of *Sports Cars Illustrated* in December 1958, it had a rev counter red-lined at 7,000 and was capable of well over 90 mph with a 20.7-second standing quarter mile. Dunlop R3 or R5 racing tyres were recommended for better wear rates while sliding on a race track, although the only other modification of note was the adoption of Castrol R vegetable-based oil in the shock absorbers to stiffen them up.

By the time *Road & Track* had a chance to test a competition Sprite, far more tuning gear was available through BMC. Their example, owned by Jim Ling, had all the equipment recommended for long-distance races such as Sebring: a 55-bhp engine, close-ratio gearbox, 4.55 rear axle, anti-roll bar, stiffer shock absorbers, wire wheels, disc front brakes, hardtop and so on, plus a silencer for road use. *Road & Track* agreed to use only 6000 rpm and returned similar performance figures to those achieved with 5983 AC in 'works' trim, an 87.4-mph maximum, 14.2-second 0–60 and 20-second standing quarter mile. *Sports Cars Illustrated* reacted vigorously by getting David Phipps to test a far more spectacular Sprite, the Speedwell coupé registered VP 7 raced by Reg Venner-Pack. This had a glass fibre hardtop and aluminium bonnet for improved aerodynamics, which made it almost indistinguishable from a Lotus Elite from some angles. It was hardly surprising—the bodywork had been designed by Frank Costin, who had worked on the Elite three years earlier, and had modified the noses of works cars along exactly the same lines! The Speedwell GT Sprite, as it was called, used similar running gear to *Road & Track*'s Sebring Sprite except that it had a 70-bhp Formula Junior engine and lighter alloy wheels with 8-inch Austin A40 drum front brakes because Speedwell were marketing them as a cheaper alternative to the disc conversion. Perhaps because of the car's lower-than-average weight, they worked perfectly efficiently, Phipps reported in *Sports Cars Illustrated*'s issue of November 1960. In this form, with an engine that ran up to 7,400 rpm on twin Amal carburettors, the Speedwell GT Sprite achieved 110.9 mph along a Belgian motorway with a 9.8-second 0–60 and a 16.5-second standing quarter mile.

The Motor then followed up with a test of a GT Sprite that was far more practical for road use. This was the car registered WXN 799 fitted with Ashley glass fibre bodywork of similar appearance to that of the Speedwell GT Sprite, and tuning gear marketed by Sprite specialist Paddy Gaston. The Ashley bonnet was unusual in that it hinged at the front and had highly-efficient interior ducting for the radiator, which allowed the engine to run cooler than normal—which was of particular advantage with highly-tuned units. *The Motor* also found, in their test on 18 January 1961, that underbonnet accessibility was much improved. The long hunch-backed hardtop was also highly aerodynamic, a quality that was not only reflected in the car's performance but in the silent way in which it was achieved, despite having a 994 cc Formula Junior engine producing 70 bhp. Wire wheels, disc front brakes, and anti-roll bar, were also fitted and a ZF limited-slip differential listed as an option. The standard 4.22 rear axle had been retained on this car, however, but it still achieved a 11.5-second 0–60 time, with a 17.8-second standing quarter mile and 97.8 mph flat out. Fuel consumption was a highly-meritorious 31 mpg, which no doubt reflected the efficiency of the bodywork. *The Motor* were also impressed with the better visibility afforded by the low-swept front of the bonnet.

Such fittings were becoming highly popular by the time John Bolster tested a famous Sebring Sprite run by John Sprinzel, who had now left Speedwell. This was the car registered PMO 200—one of several to bear that number—that Sprinzel had taken to a class six win in the RAC Rally in November 1960 and Pat Moss had raced in exactly the same form at Brands Hatch the following Boxing Day. In fact, the car was unaltered when Bolster tested it for *Autosport* on 10 February 1961. It had a glass fibre bonnet, aluminium doors and body, and glass fibre hard top using the standard windscreen and sidescreens in a similar number to the Ashley top. More weight was saved by fitting glass fibre seats. In rally form, Sprinzel's Sebring Sprite was fitted with a 62-bhp engine that was capable of 7,000 rpm and standard gear ratios, with wire wheels and disc brakes. Bolster commented:

> 'The track of the Sebring has been increased by the offset spoking of the wheels. This gives improved stability and it also alters the steering geometry by increasing the centre-point distance. The result is a controllability on wet roads which can only be described as phenomenal, but the very sensitivity which confers this exceptional handling also causes every bump to be felt at the wheel. Thus, although the car is completely stable and does not deviate, a very bumpy road may tend to punish the driver's wrists. You can't have it both ways and the enthusiast will revel in the delightfully sensitive steering, which seems to allow him to "feel" the road surface.'

A sister car, a Sprinzel Sprite registered S 221, that Stirling Moss raced at Sebring in 1961, was tested by *The Autocar* in full-race form with an 80-bhp Formula Junior engine and close ratio gearbox from a Mark II Sprite. It also had the 4.875:1 rear axle ratio that was popular for short British circuits in place of the normal 4.55, with wire wheels, disc front brakes, anti-roll bar and competition dampers. The bodywork was extensively lightened with a glass fibre

Travel-stained, but willing, the Spridget registered 250 DOL still proved to be a good performer for *Motor Sport* and *The Motor*.

bonnet and aluminium Costin-style hardtop besides the alloy tail and doors. In this form, with its 12-gallon tank half full and a spare wheel in place, it weighed 11.75 cwt—2 cwt less than a standard hardtop Sprite. The interior was rudimentary to say the least with both the road and the rear axle visible through gaps around the rear-mounted battery. *The Autocar* said in their issue of 25 August 1961:

'The first thing one notices as soon as the engine starts is the noise. Even the most hardened extrovert would be embarrassed by the amount of exhaust noise from this car ... In town, the car was a slight nuisance, as it was inclined to overheat and even the soft plugs started to misfire. It also became very warm in the cockpit and one sat in a mist of Castrol R fumes—very intoxicating for the diehard enthusiasts. Surprisingly enough, the engine was remarkably tractable, and one could potter along at relatively low engine speeds. Full power from the engine was not available under 5,000 rpm, but it then continued right through to 7,00 rpm.'

With a 7,200-rpm rev limit, *The Autocar* recorded a 100 mph maximum on the low rear axle ratio with a 17.8-second standing quarter mile and a 10.8-second 0–60 mph

Formula Junior was reaching its peak in the early 1960s with a great deal of time and money being spent on engine development—to the advantage of the Sprite! By the time Patrick McNally tested a Sprinzel Sprite raced by David Siegle-Morris for the 26 January 1962 issue of *Autosport*, it had an engine developing 88 bhp at 7,500 rpm with a limit in excess of 8,000. Providing you kept the revs between 5,500 and 7,500, the performance of this car, registered D 20, was startling. In substantially the same trim as *The Autocar*'s Sebring Sprite, and on the same low axle ratio, it recorded a 105.8-mph maximum speed with an 8.2-second 0–60 and a 16.8-second standing quarter mile. The price, incidentally, was about double that of a standard Sprite, the extra £700 being divided almost equally between the engine and the bodywork.

The First Spridgets

The Autocar was the first magazine to test the restyled Sprite on 2 June 1961, noting that many of the criticisms about the earlier car had now been remedied. Special praise was reserved for the luggage boot lid, on which they reported in thoroughly jingoistic vein:

'Without doubt one of the greatest improvements is the alteration of the boot for external access—a feature that everyone has clamoured for since the Sprite was first introduced. That the car now has a completely lockable compartment greatly increases its potential for touring abroad.'

The extra power and close ratio gearbox improved the performance only slightly, however, because of the extra weight of their hardtop model, registered 250 DOL. The 0–60 time was 19.8 seconds with a 21.8-second standing start quarter mile and top speed of 85.5 mph—6 mph less in open form. Fuel consumption was about the same at 33 mpg overall. They also commented on the revised structure:

'As well as a slight increase in weight there has been a small change in its distribution. There is proportionately less weight on the front wheels than previously. This has not appreciably altered the handling characteristics of the car, although it has probably aggravated the tendency of the rear wheels to steer the car when cornering. It is characteristic of this type of suspension that the flattening of the outer rear spring and the arching of the inner one bring the axle out of line with the chassis and create a mild oversteer. As the car is straightened after a corner the reverse effect is also noticed.

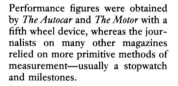

Performance figures were obtained by *The Autocar* and *The Motor* with a fifth wheel device, whereas the journalists on many other magazines relied on more primitive methods of measurement—usually a stopwatch and milestones.

'Nearly everyone who drove the car thought that the springing felt softer than previously, although according to the makers no changes have been made. Perhaps the additional weight reacting against the springs results in a slightly greater suspension movement.'

The Motor then recorded performance figures nearly as good with 250 DOL on 12 July 1961, before commenting:

'With the hood raised or with the unlined plastic hardtop in place, road and wind noise seem to echo and make this a noisy car at any but low speeds, the optional radio being of little use above 30 mph and sustained conversation scarcely practicable above 60 mph. While the engine had a healthy bark when working, the exhaust is not unreasonably noisy save for a rather conspicuous rasp on the overrun from high speeds. Some sound absorbing material might make this a less tiring car for long journeys, but it could be reasonably claimed that a car which is seldom going quite as fast as it seems is inherently safe ...

'Although the Mark II Sprite has not quite the simple charm of its predecessors, its better bodywork, increased power and still remarkable fuel economy make it better value for money than ever before.'

The Motor also had an opportunity to try an MG Midget, registered YJB 217, for the same issue, saying:

'The front floor covering of mottled plastic instead of rubbed rubber, and felt bonded to the underside of this plastic seems to do a useful noise-reducing job at speeds below 45 mph. Another MG refinement concerns the rigid sidescreens, in which both front and rear halves of the window can slide open, instead of only the rear halves.'

The earlier Mark II Sprites were frequently fitted with the 'old-style' hardtops that could be readily identified by this large oval rear window.

For some strange reason, Mark I Midgets were far more often fitted with the new, more angular, hardtop.

Many of the works competition, press fleet, and advertising cars, carried a YJB registration mark—that of the nearest local taxation office to Abingdon.

The new Midget proved to be slightly slower than the Sprite, particularly on acceleration, when tested by *The Motor*, but fractionally faster when *The Autocar* tried it in hardtop form for their issue of 18 August 1961, highlighting how critical the state of tune could be. This car was also fitted with an upholstered rear squab which *The Autocar* considered adequate for two children if the front seats were pushed well forward.

Similar performance figures were recorded for the new Sprite in *Car and Driver*—the American successor to *Sports Cars Illustrated*—in their July 1961 issue before *Road & Track* gave the car an extensive test in August 1961. They thoroughly approved of the styling changes save for the odd detail:

'To reduce drumming in the rear fender panel, the rear wheel cutout is flared slightly (for stiffening purposes), which looks odd only because this wasn't done at the front.

'The big news at the rear end of the Sprite is the trunk lid. It is lockable too, and uses a separate key. As at the hood [bonnet] there is a rod to prop the lid open, though here it is less satisfactory . . . such as when one arm is loaded down.

'The spare tyre and wheel lie flat on the floor, taking up most of the floor area despite their small size. The gas tank is bolted to the bottom of the trunk's flat floor and seems lost in all that space, shared only with the diminutive muffler. With all the retooling for externals, surely it wouldn't have been too much to redesign the floor and the gas tank to maximise the available trunk space. Still, the Mark II is a vast improvement, merely because the access is so much better, and you can pack things in all those small nooks and crannies because you can at least see them now.

'For a car that still has no ashtray, there is the surprising total of five satchels provided for storing items in the trunk. Two are of vinyl plastic, one contains the jack, another the side curtains (a partition separates the pair, giving full protection to the soft plastic windows). A small cloth bag carries the tools, a large one the folded top. A boomerang-shaped leatherette bag, heavily lined with rough felt, carries the tubular top-bows which now split on the car's centreline to ease storage (but requires an assistant to install quickly). When all these items are dropped casually into the trunk, one may well wonder where the luggage is going to go. However, there's a nook or a hook for each one and the result is a tidy trunk without a mess of rattles . . .

'Cockpit ventilation in the Sprite seems to have just happened. Fully open, it's fun as can be and the front seat is well protected, apparently by the door's high sides. But when the top is up, there is a steady blast on the side of your head. With the sidescreens on, it's very snug and the solitary fault is that the effective heater-ventilator has no cockpit control over temperature . . .

'It offers more fun per dollar than anything we have driven for a long time.'

The floppy rubber mats of the Mark II Sprite were continued under the seats—which had detachable squabs to make cleaning easier.

Sliding sidescreens became a standard fitting with a similar hood to that of the Mark I Sprite—and pressed steel roadwheels were frequently concealed by these Rimbellishers.

The Autocar considered that the optional rear squab was adequate for children—of a size not specified—providing that the seats were moved well forward. If they were not, as this picture shows, there was absolutely no legroom. The new seatbelt mounting bolts can also be seen in this picture, with one on the inside of the sill at the back of the seat, and two on top of the wheelarch.

Car and Driver were equally enthusiastic over the Midget when they tested it in February 1962, reporting that one fan said: 'It's as if the TD were reincarnated!' To this reaction they added the comment:

'The statement is valid up to a point. The car has the same handy feel of the last of the T's, but has more functional features, a slightly less powerful engine which nevertheless gives better performance and a unitized body that's solid and rattle-free. The cockpit of the new car has greater legroom and feels less restrictive, even with the top up. The seats are more comfortable and a third person can be accommodated in the area behind the seats … The trunk is a useful feature. Its shape and size are more practical than that of even the larger MGB.'

The First Modified Spridgets

Naturally the tuning firms were quick to market conversions for the Spridgets, which varied so little mechanically from the original Sprite. Speedwell's ultimate road car, tested by *The Autocar* on 29 June 1962, was positively festooned with gadgets. This car, registered 254 CGT, had an alloy cylinder head, giving an 11:1 compression ratio, Speedwell CS2 camshaft, modified valve gear, twin Amal carburettors, special exhaust system, and a 4.55:1 rear axle ratio. In addition, it had an anti-roll bar, oil cooler, wire wheels, special seats and instruments, Healey prototype-style bonnet air scoop, and exterior door handles. Drum brakes were retained with hard linings. *The Autocar* reported:

'At low engine speeds, the modified car is rather slower than the standard Sprite. As the engine speed increases, the full advantage of the conversion makes itself felt, and the performance is pleasantly brisk. Nearly 2 secs fewer are required to cover the standing quarter mile, and this level of

The Dick Jacobs Midget, registered 770 BJB, as tested by George Phillips of *Autosport*, hard on the tail of a Ferrari 250GTO in the 1963 Tourist Trophy race at Goodwood.

Its sister car, 771 BJB, used the same special bodywork with an aerodynamic nose based on the shape of the EX181 record car. The windscreen surround was like that of the Sebring Sprites, except that it was of a more standard shape.

performance continues to about 85 mph ... Above this the acceleration dies away and the engine runs out of power at about 90 mph. The car is at its best on twisty roads away from built-up areas where the crisp exhaust note will not offend. Under these conditions, and making full use of the 74 mph maximum in third gear, the car was terrific fun to drive and handled exceptionally well.'

A 90-mph maximum speed was recorded with a 15.2-second 0–60 , 19.9-second standing quarter mile and fuel consumption estimated at 30 mpg. The brakes stood up to this well and features *The Autocar* liked particularly included the seats and exterior door handles.

It was back to the really hot Sprites when John Bolster had the opportunity to test a new model tuned by Healeys for *Autosport* on 31 August 1962. This car, registered 925 CNX, had a 997-cc engine, special large valve alloy cylinder head, twin 1.5-inch SU carburettors, fabricated exhaust system, high-compression pistons, competition camshaft and distributor, lightened flywheel and nine-spring clutch, besides wire wheels and disc brakes all round, a 4.55 rear axle and glass fibre hardtop. It oiled one plug in traffic ... but went up to 101.5 mph at nearly 8,000 rpm with a 0–60 time that Bolster recorded as 10 seconds. And then *The Autocar* made 925 CNX go even quicker! Their test on 26 October 1962 achieved a top speed of 104 mph with a 12.4-second 0–60, and 18.2-second standing quarter mile, with no less than 28 mpg! But they added this cautionary note of a conversion that cost £400 and took the total price of the car beyond £1,000:

'Unfortunately low-speed tractability has been forfeited to achieve high performance. The combination of poor torque at low engine speeds, a harsh competition clutch, plus undue transmission slack, demanded firm but gentle clutch and accelerator co-ordination to ensure a smooth getaway. On the move, the same factors precluded the use of less than 2,500 rpm in any gear, so that local journeys in built-up areas were made mostly in second gear.'

The 1,100 cc Midget registered 496 CJB, on the other hand, aroused a much more appreciative reaction from Blain.

Two years later, Janos Odor and Dave Bowns, who had worked for Daniel Richmond at the highly-respected Downton Engineering, produced a £40 conversion for the 948-cc Spridget that was an absolute bargain. With no more than a modified cylinder head, special manifolds and rejetted carburettors, their Sprite proved to be capable of 95 mph with an 18.2-second 0–60 and a superbly clean pick-up from 750 rpm to 7,000 when tested by Patrick McNally for *Autosport* on 17 May 1963. It was no small wonder that their firm, Janspeed, was to become one of the most successful in this field, with many others going out of business. Their products were simply far better value for money.

Meanwhile *Autosport*'s chief photographer, George Phillips, who used to race MGs at Le Mans, had managed to borrow one of Dick Jacob's special Midgets—the car registered 770 BJB—for a test in the issue of 14 December 1962. This highly successful GT racer had an Abingdon-tuned 979-cc engine with special camshaft, 10:1 compression ratio cylinder head, and single 45DCOE Weber carburettor, of which Phillips said:

'Although the engine is very potent, it is quite reasonable in its demands. For example, on Champion 63Rs, the plug on which it actually races, Esso Golden fuel will never produce a pink and Castrol R keeps everything whirring merrily round close to the 8,000 rpm mark with no complaints.'

So far as suspension was concerned, it had softer rear springs, with Aeon

The dashboard and interior failed to impress Mr Blain, however...

But the 1100 Spridget registered 747 GON received a polite review from *The Motor*...

rubber bump stops, stiffer-set Armstrong competition dampers, and a heavier
front anti-roll bar—which gave it normal Sprite handling, according to Phillips.
Its streamlined alloy bonnet with a tiny air intake and long fastback hardtop
grated onto the normal steel floorpan, made quite a difference, however. Phillips
wrote:

> '0–30 took just 2.2 seconds, 0–50 was 5.8 secs, while 7.9 secs was enough
> to reach 60. It was from there on, I think, that the body really started to
> help, as 70 mph took a mere 10.2 secs, and 80 13 flat ... That standing
> quarter mile worked out at 16.2 secs.'

This car also achieved 111.9 mph on a 4.875 rear axle!

The Healey family had long been campaigning for a more flexible high-
performance engine like that used in sports racing cars to be made available for
the Sprite. The Coventry Climax 1100 unit was ideal in some respects because it
was also lighter—although it was very expensive by BMC standards. BMC were
also adamant that they did not want to see anybody else's engine in what
amounted to a works Sprite—but it did not take long for world champion racing
driver Jack Brabham to develop a conversion using the similar 1220 cc overhead
cam all alloy Climax unit from the Lotus Elite for the Midget. He had a great
deal of experience in fitting these units to Triumph Heralds, and particularly in
developing mountings that minimised vibrations that had become notorious with
this unit in some adaptations. It was an expensive transformation, at £360
including disc front brakes, but an uncommonly good one, giving Brabham's
demonstrator, registered 751 VPF, a top speed of 107 mph, soft top up, with a 9-
second 0–60, and 16.4-second standing quarter mile. But that was not the
whole story as John Bolster told in *Autosport* on 29 December 1961:

> 'The engine is more flexible than the unit it replaces, and will propel the
> car at 15 mph in top gear without protest. If flexibility is one aspect of the
> engine, an appetite for high revolutions is an even more pronounced
> characteristic. When hurrying, one normally changes up at 6,500 rpm, and
> at this speed the short-stroke unit is completely unstressed.
>
> 'Even more impressive is the acceleration through the gears. The rear
> axle of the test car was much less inclined to tramp than is usually the case
> with Sprites, in spite of the vastly greater power available (83 bhp). This is
> apparently due to the improved weight distribution.'

Bolster went on to emphasise what a difference the Climax engine made to
the Midget ... but in not much more than a year, supplies were to run out as
Lotus used up their initial order and went on to cheaper Ford-based units.

Then in March 1963, long after the revised 1100 cc Spridgets had been
introduced, a new British monthly magazine *small car*, had the opportunity to test
a 948-cc Sprite with a Nerus conversion in conjunction with a Turner 1500 kit
car using a power unit from the same tuner. Their evaluation of the Sprite was
especially significant where it dealt with the basic car, registered 3327 FN,
which was unaltered apart from a new cylinder head. If the conversion was

Even Bill Boddy, locked in memories of pre-war motoring, found the sliding Perspex screens inconvenient.

relatively mild, the comments of assistant editor Doug Blain were distinctly biting. He said:

'Both cars are traditional in layout in that they have their engines surrounded by seas of waste space ahead of the two occupants, who sit with their legs stretched right out well aft of the wheelbase centre point. A low bootline in each case leaves little room for luggage above or behind the rear axle, which is rigid in the (um) traditional manner ...

'Neither car is visually outstanding. The Sprite suffers from lack of character; its original predecessor had a bug-eyed look that took it too far the other way, but in getting around old objections without sacrificing too many costly body dies, BMC has smoothed its smallest sports car into a square-ended blob which totally lacks the excitement of line we are told younger buyers go for. Another disadvantage of the revised body is that it makes access to the engine normally difficult instead of outstandingly easy ...

'Our principal complaint, assuming Sprite buyers are dedicated enough to stomach starkness at this price, is with the disposition of the controls that are supposed to bring the driver his pleasure in having such a car. The wheel is so close to the seat that not even a midget can get far enough back to swing his arms. The gear lever is so high and so close that an elbow hook would be more convenient for shifting than a hand. The handbrake (on this right-hand-drive car) is obviously meant for the passenger rather than the driver, although we guess it has its uses for bachelor types that way. And finally the placement of the pedals makes it impossible to use them except by pumping your whole leg from the thigh—a procedure guaranteed (a) to bring muscle fatigue and (b) to scuff the backs of any pair of shoes yet cobbled ...

'Is it worth putting up with all these miseries just to own a fast open car? The advent of the hot small mass-production saloon (Cooper Mini, Lotus Cortina) and the rise of the baby GT (Ogle, Deep Sanderson) has meant that lots of buyers are getting tempted to forget the open bit and buy fast, comfortable, quiet, windproof cars instead. So are we.'

Motor Sport discovered that the timing gear on the Nerus Sprite registered 8245 FN made only a marginal difference.

Motor's half-elliptic Midget registered AJB 599B, went down well with the testers, who were especially appreciative of its extra performance, better cornering and some aspects of its revised interior.

The Early 1100-cc Spridgets

Blain then went on to explain in a test of a standard 1100 Midget in *small car* in July 1963 that he had been writing in a relative manner. When he raved over the handling of a Morris 1100, it was in comparison with that of other small saloons; likewise, when he said the Spridgets felt tail happy it was in relation to other small sporting vehicles. Of the changes made to the 1,100 cc model, registered 496 CJB, he said:

> 'Frankly, from our point of view, they very nearly transform the car. Never have we known so few changes to make such an improvement in a model's appeal. Oddly enough the difference in performance is the one you notice least ... acceleration through the gears takes rather less to 40 mph and less

again to 60 mph: enough to make a difference to your point-to-point average even though the Spridget is still anything but a winner away from the lights. The precisely calibrated dashboard rev counter (still the only practical reason we can see for buying a Midget and not a Sprite, which had dreadful instruments) has an orange sector from 5500 rpm to 6000 rpm and a red one from there on ...

'Of far more practical day-to-day use than the extra mechanical urge is the revised gearbox, which above all accounts for the fact that the Sprite is suddenly driveable. It has the same higher and closer ratios that distinguished the 948 cc Spridgets from their pop-eyed and rather depressing ancestors, but without the maddening clunks and graunches that greeted every attempt at a semi-smart shift. Instead of a misery it has become a pleasure to change gear really quickly in the latest car. Our only regret is that first, pleasantly high and eminently useable as it is, should have remained unsynchonised and therefore out of reach to all but the bravest and most skilled. Oh, and it would be nice not to have to put up with all the unaccountable whining and grumbling that still gets past the casing.

'The new brakes are an equally welcome improvement from a real driver's point of view. Thrashing old Spridgets through the lanes, you often got the feeling that there may be nothing there the next time you stepped on the pedal, and occasionally after a really earnest mile or two there wasn't. This time we tried equally hard to make the brakes disappear. We failed.

'We didn't think much of the new cockpit arrangements. The so-called crash padding strikes us (ha-ha) as an elaborate practical joke since it seems to be fastened on below the bottom of the dash with skinny little metal brackets that wouldn't stop a stone ...

'In all, if social considerations or That Ole Fangio Feeling dictate that you must own a small, cheap sports car then we see no reason why this one shouldn't keep you quiet for a bit.'

The window winders and quarter lights that went with the new, lighter, and more airy, hardtop made the Spridget much more civilised.

The old-style doors with wide cut-outs did give more elbow room, however. Later examples, such as the one illustrated, even went so far as to have a knob on their door handle to make inadvertent contact with the elbow less painful.

As Blain presented an alternative view of the Spridget, the rest of the motoring Press stuck to their established formulae. *The Motor* said the new engine 'seemed appreciably quieter and less fussy than previous models' in their test of an 1100 Sprite on 5 December 1962. In less than favourable conditions, their car, registered 747 GON, managed 87.8 mph, with a 16.6-second 0–60 and 20.9-second standing quarter mile, with no more than 6,000 rpm being used. Nevertheless, *The Motor* felt that this Sprite was now a shade undergeared on its standard 4.22 rear axle ratio. On the other hand, it was only able to restart on a 1-in-3 gradient by having its clutch slipped at high revs! But at least the new clutch took such punishment, whereas it was felt that the old one would surely have wilted ... *The Motor* also noted that the new baulk ring synchromesh could no longer be beaten by very rapid shifts, and so far as the new brakes were concerned, they were much lighter and inspired confidence. The better upholstery was also praised—but not the draughty sidescreens.

They also highlighted for the first time a problem with the fresh air ventilation system where the intake pipe behind the radiator grille could suck in poisonous fumes from the exhaust pipes of other vehicles while at a standstill in heavy traffic jams. *Motor Sport* found a solution to this problem in their test of a Midget 1100 in April 1965. They recommended pulling out the heater control knob to close the nose intake while operating the interior fan to recirculate air inside. Bill Boddy, editor of *Motor Sport*, also tested two Triumph Spitfires in the same issue and had this to say about their Midget, registered 496 CJB:

'After the Triumph Spitfire, the MG Midget at first gives the impression of being a toy, very low, very small, rather difficult to see out of with the hood up, rough and noisy. After a day's motoring in it I had considerably revised this opinion, and at the end of a lengthy test I was a firm Midget enthusiast, for this MG, no less than the better of its predecessors, feels "all in one piece" is responsive, sprightly and very quick about the place, moderately comfortable, and essentially safe.

'It is perhaps "less of a car" than the Spitfire, more difficult to get into and out of with the hood up. Its sliding Perspex side windows, instead of wind-up glass windows and a hood that tends to drum and, in spite of ingenious telescopic sticks, is not particularly easy to erect, are not altogether endearing. Casual minor controls, such as manually-cancelling indicators operated by a fascia flick-switch, inaccurate instruments and doors that lack exterior handles, so that, if the sliding sidescreens freeze up, entry to the MG poses a problem the solution of which, to say the least, looks like burglary, make a price of £42 below that charged for the Triumph seem disadvantageously disporportionate. However, on longer acquaintance this latest of a long line of MG Midgets comes over as a very likeable and attractive little car. Everything about it tends to be simple, yet adequate.'

He then went on to extol the virtues of the Midget, recording similar performance figures to those of *The Motor*, which made it fractionally slower

Apart from the general proportions, the Le Mans Sprites, as tested by John Blunsden for *Motor Racing*, looked quite unlike normal cars because of their special bodywork—but in reality, they were surprisingly similar under the skin.

than the 1,147 cc Spitfire. But it was significant that Boddy did not criticise the Spitfire's swing axle rear suspension, which made its handling so inferior to that of a Spridget. Triumph were eventually forced to change their cost-cutting independent rear suspension—but at the time of the Spitfire's introduction in 1962 its deficiencies were not apparent to many people.

Mike Twite of *Motor Sport* then tested the Midget 747 GON for the next issue in May 1963 because he normally drove a Frogeye, and made these illuminating comments:

'Most owners of the earlier model feel that the latest car has "gone soft" and this is true to a great extent, for on the 1098 cc version a great deal of unnecessary trim has been added ...

'However, for the average sports car buyer who intends to use the car only on the road the new model is probably a better proposition ... The handling is very similar, with perhaps a little more roll being apparent, but it can still be thrown about in a very enterprising manner ...

'Last year I compared the Sprite unfavourably with the Mini-Cooper ... but in the intervening 12 months I have mellowed slightly as well as having a good deal more experience with the Cooper, and while giving it full marks for speed and handling I can well see why many people still stick to the arms-stretch driving position, open-air motoring and the safe and uncomplicated handling of the Sprite.'

Autocar eventually tested Blain's 1100 Midget, 496 CJB, in hardtop form for their issue of 8 November 1963. By then it was more than a year old—which was unusual for a road-test car—and had covered 16,000 miles. With these factors in mind, *Autocar* were impressed with how the Midget had stood up to the hard usage normally accorded to a Press car. It seemed as though it needed a decoke, but still did 89 mph and 29 mpg. *Autocar* echoed every good sentiment that had been expressed about Spridgets, but also felt that it was about time the detail fittings were improved in specification—notably so far as locking was concerned. Such thoughts were shared by *Road & Track* in their test of an 1100 Sprite in August 1963, with the addition of a welcome for the interior carpets to replace the previous 'unborn Gila monster hide.'

Modified Early 1100 Spridgets

Many new firms joined the tuning business as conversions for the Mini and mechanically-similar Spridget became more and more popular. For a variety of reasons, varying from bad luck to bad engineering, only a few survived. A good example of the problems that could beset a tuner was shown when a private owner submitted a Sprite for test by *Autocar*. This car, registered 690 CWX, had been converted for driving tests using equipment supplied by Forspeed, including a special exhaust system, large-valve cylinder head and 45DCOE Weber carburettor. *Autocar*, reporting on 26 April 1963, were not impressed. They said:

'This exhaust system did little, if any, silencing and made the car a continual source of embarrassment even on the open road. For an owner interested in rallying, the noise level would certainly preclude the car from being passed by the start scrutineers, and it was immediately classified as a boy's racer likely to incur the wrath of the police. On the road, the Sprite was fairly tractable, but care had to be taken when accelerating from low speeds in a high gear, since an unrestrained dab on the throttle caused an over-rich mixture which wetted the plugs ... accelerations from a standing start were seriously affected by excessive clutch slip. No modifications had been made to the Sprite's suspension, but Michelin X tyres had been fitted. As supplied to us, the pressures had been set to equal values of 27 psi all round despite Michelin's recommendations of 20 psi front and 30 psi rear. The result was extreme oversteer, which was most disconcerting ... Even at the recommended pressures the car was decidedly twitchy and at maximum speed one did not feel completely at ease.'

Bolster had a far happier time when Speedwell's 1961 Sprite, 254 CGT, turned up for a test in *Autosport* on 26 July 1963. By then it had a 89 bhp Weber-carburetted engine that was in fact a 948 cc unit bored out to 1,080 cc to retain the shorter stroke for high revs. In contrast to the Forspeed car, it had a very quiet, tuned-length, exhaust system and made the car more than 10 mph faster at 105.8 mph with a 0–60 of 9.1 seconds and standing quarter mile of 16.7 seconds. There was also a contrast in the price of the conversion ... nearly four times as much at £250. In addition, the Speedwell car had a 'Monza' glass fibre bonnet similar to that of the Sebring Sprites, but with an even longer nose, and one of Speedwell's latest lines at the time, a rather angular works-style 'Clubman' glass fibre hardtop of which Bolster said:

> 'The tail section of the current Midget is not well streamlined and even better results can be obtained with an early Sprite shell.'

Motor Sport then tested an 1100 cc Sprite, registered 8245 FN, in December 1963 with a large valve cylinder head, modified manifolds, and 1.5-inch SU carburettors by Nerus, who concentrated mainly on engine work rather than complete conversions. This tuning gear, which cost £70, made only a marginal difference at 96 mph flat out with a 0–60 of 14.7 seconds and standing start of 19.5 seconds.

Late 1100 Spridgets

The changes to the first half-elliptic sprung Spridgets was welcomed by the motoring magazines. 'The new Sprite is faster, holds the road better, rides more comfortably and is more habitable,' said *Autocar* in their test on 24 April 1964. Although the power was up only 3 bhp, and torque remained the same, their car,

Road & Track were suitably impressed with the Spridget's new hood.

The 1,275 cc Sprite continued to be very popular despite 'a ride which is firm by modern standards' in 1967— 'but which would have been considered unusually soft in the Mark I Sprite era,' said *Motor*.

registered AJB 342B, was 2 mph faster at 91.8 mph, with much better acceleration, taking only 14.5 seconds for the 0–60, and 19.4 seconds for the standing quarter mile. They added:

'The measure of the Sprite's progress is emphasized by comparing it with its larger-engined stablemates of earlier years. Although having a considerably lower maximum speed than the 1.5 litre MGAs, its figures beat any of them except the twin cam up to 80 mph, and it is quicker to 60 mph than the first of the 1600s tried out in 1959 ... Added to this agility the Sprite's compact dimensions, its lightning reactions to the controls and a new standard of roadholding, and it is clear that the car is potentially one of the quickest means of reaching B from A on British country roads ...

'From the driver's viewpoint, the most significant of all the Sprite's modifications is the substitution of conventional half-elliptic rear springs for the previous quarter elliptics. The theoretical advantages of reduced unsprung weight (since the mounting brackets on the axle casing are much simpler and lighter) and better location of the axle are fully borne out in practice. The half-elliptics allow more travel at a softer rate, which means improved comfort and a reduction in axle hop over bad surfaces; more important, they cut out "rear-wheel steering" and the over-sensitivity of control that were criticized in previous Sprites. Strong side winds or indifferent surfaces no longer call for concentration to keep it on course. This is a really important contribution to one's peace of mind and physical relaxation on long runs.'

Motor, like *Autocar* having dropped the *The* from their title for trendy reasons, were equally appreciative of the modernisation of the Spridget when they tested a Midget registered AJB 599B, on 16 May 1964. They commented:

'One attraction of a small sports car like the Midget is its easy adaptability to the weather. Performance and handling are big considerations, and when the same car can offer all, so much the better. The Midget, and the Sprite before it, have always been praised for their handling, particularly for the accuracy and sensitive feel in the steering. Criticism often aimed at the Mark I Sprite (effectively the Mark 0 Midget) was that its performance did not match its looks.

'The Mark I Midget changed a lot of that, especially when the 1098 cc engine came along; and now the Mark II car has found a little more power still at slightly higher revs; enough to improve the 0–60 mph time from 16.6 seconds to 14.9, compared with the 1100 Sprite we tested. In top gear the 20–40 time is slightly worse, the 30–50 about the same while 40–60 times and beyond are distinctly better, emphasizing the raised power curve due to larger inlet valves and revised cylinder head. Although the performance figures deny it, this car does not feel any less tractable and it is quite content to potter gently.

'These, however, are not the biggest changes. Wind-up windows, lockable doors and a heater are held by the early Sprite generation to detract from the original fresh air sports character. Such objection to progress is quite unfounded; the changes widen the potential market of the Midget to include many differing ages and mentalities, and either sex. The original enthusiast, probably single (there is room for little more than a portable cot behind the seats), will like the improvement in cornering stability given by semi-elliptic instead of quarter leaf springs at the rear.

'Splendid controllability, good performance and nice lines make the Midget fun, and it has room for a reasonable amount of luggage behind the seats and in the boot. Big people will find it a difficult fit, and knees splayed round the steering wheel will foul the window winder; the space now occupied by the window mechanism has removed the door pocket space (which previously provided extra elbow room) to cramp the tall man still further.

'If you still buy a sports car primarily for sport, the Midget has plenty of virtues to counteract these shortcomings.'

Bill Boddy then tested the same Midget for *Motor Sport* in October 1964. He noted that the 'S' versions of the Mini-Cooper could outperform it, although they cost 10–20 per cent more, and then commented:

'What can I say about this ever-popular little car? It has no particular individuality, is inferior to a Mini in ride and roadholding, and therefore under certain circumstances less rapid on a journey ...

'Yet the demand for such a sports model is unabated—for many days I hardly saw the car, because my eldest daughter resolutely refused to be parted from it.

'The MG Midget is essentially a car for the younger generation. Getting in and out necessitates some rather jack-knife contortions for the old but as so many women wear trousers these days, this is probably no deterrent, although now that girls favour skintight slacks (and I'm not complaining) there would seem to be some danger of a split.'

The revised Sprite came in for a lot of praise from Blain when he tried one registered FMP 884B for *small car* in October 1964, with a mark one Spitfire for comparison. Although the Spitfire's styling appealed more to Blain, the Sprite came out on top by a considerable margin as the better car, chiefly due to its superior handling. He said of the Sprite:

'The new rear suspension turns BMC's baby into an exceedingly quick and safe car for belting through the lanes. Its handling is still more or less what you make it, but the initial understeer is much less noticeable than before and the tail far less inclined to hang itself out suddenly and dramatically. In the faster bends you can simply select your line, apply enough power (but not too much, or you'll get yourself crossed up for no reason) and let the car sail through four-square without drama. In slower corners, it's sometimes fun to give the throttle a jab and then jerk the lightning-quick steering round to catch the playfully wagging tail, but again you'll find you go through faster if you use a gentler technique. How fast is faster? Well, early Sprites may have had to give best in, say, a typical roundabout to a well-driven Mini but we believe this latest model will outcorner a Mini and remain as completely controllable right up to the limit as most production car rivals. Our only reservation concerns body roll, which is still marked for a sports car and which can at times catch you out if you need to change direction in a hurry.'

The Spitfire, with its well-known propensity for tucking one rear wheel under in extreme circumstances, proved tricky here. Blain also considered the Sprite's gearing—although slightly too low in first and second, to be better—and the seats, instruments, and interior generally to be better on the Sprite, if still primitive. Apart from higher maximum speeds in first and second gear, the performance of the cars was about the same, although the Spitfire was slightly superior on fuel consumption.

Much the same feelings were echoed by *Cars and Car Conversions*, which had replaced *Cars Illustrated*, in their issue of October 1965, with the added comment:

'You can't expect everything on a car that only costs just over six hundred quid, of course, but the Sprite seems to have most things.'

Modified Late Model 1100 Spridgets

Cars and Car Conversions also managed to test a privately-owned and particularly-impressive 1,100 cc Taurus-converted Sprite in March 1969. This car had a 9.5:1 compression ratio gas-flowed big-valve cylinder head that cost only £28 exchange, Cooper S distributor and SU carburettors—but its top speed was no less than 101 mph with the hood down! It also achieved an 11.3-second 0–60 time, an 18.5-second standing quarter mile and had enough torque to tow a broken down Triumph TR4. Apart from being fitted with wire wheels, and Koni dampers and Aeon bump stops at the back, the rest of the car was virtually standard. It had been fitted with Car Hood Company Rallye seats, however, which did wonders at transforming the 'Gnome's Crouch' driving position, said the magazine, affectionately known as *Triple C.*

Le Mans Sprites

John Blunsden had the opportunity for a brief test in two works Sprites built for the 1965 Le Mans race. They had been bought by Richard Groves for international competition in 1966, one being fitted with a 1,098-cc Formula Junior engine and the other retaining its 1,293-cc unit. Initially, Blunsden was surprised to find how standard the cars were despite their special bodywork of vastly altered appearance. Both had been fitted with 4.5 rear axle ratios in place of the 4.2 used at Le Mans, in conjunction with standard BMC competition gearboxes. Blunsden reported for *Motor Racing* in June 1966:

> 'Life was that little bit easier in the large-engine car through the corners. In overall lap times the two cars appeared to be over three seconds apart, most of which would be accounted for by engine power. Without too much difficulty, we found the 1,293 cc Sprite good for a 62-second lap on the day, and with the stronger dampers on the rear improved stability should find a little more time. This is a very satisfactory result for a car which makes no pretensions of being one of the "paper mache brigade" for club racing. It is designed, above all, to go and keep going, and although it may stand little chance in terms of all-out performance against the more exotic (and much more expensive) Abarths, its reliability factor must surely enable it to scoop up some useful prizes during the coming season of endurance races.'

Early 1275-cc Spridgets

After a brief run in December 1966 in a 1,275 cc Midget, registered DWL 557D, that was still too stiff to show its full performance, *CAR*, which had taken over from *small car*, had a second opportunity to compare the latest lines in Spitfires and Sprites in May 1967. The Spitfire—Mark III—was much appreciated for its improved appearance, and *CAR* noted that its more modern driving position now showed how old-fashioned that of the Sprite had become. But despite radial ply tyres and wider-tracked wire wheels, the Spitfire's handling was as tricky as ever. The Sprite, on the other hand, had an inferior ride—but its gearbox was far more fun and above all, it was so much safer.

Road & Track then went on to compare a Midget and a Spitfire Mark III in a test in September 1967. They liked the Midget's new hood, saying 'It is now a proper convertible top that goes up and down easily and is a great improvement over the roadster-style build-it-yourself top', before discovering that the Spitfire was the faster car with a 100-mph top speed and 13.6-second 0–60 mph against 93 and 14.7. While in the mood for comparison tests, they also lined up a Sprite against another Spitfire, and a Datsun 1600 and Fiat 850 Spider in October 1968, with two young college students as judges. *Road & Track* reported:

> 'In general, they see the basic sports car as a "beginner" car for many 16-to-20-year-old drivers; the first car many of them will own, the car they will be looking forward to as soon as they get their driver's licences. One of the most appealing features of these cars is cost, as might be expected. These are the lowest priced sports cars on the market; cheapest in original outlay, moderate in operating cost, relatively inexpensive to keep in repair. Also of fundamental importance is the fact that they are far more likely to receive parental approval than either an in-car like a wide-tracked, drag-slicked musclecar or a more powerful sports car. "My folks didn't bat an eyelid when I talked about getting a Fiat," said Jay, "But when I mentioned Porsche, boy, they went right to the ceiling." It is also of some importance that insurance companies are slightly less appalled at young drivers in basic sports cars than machines of superior power.'

How the times have changed ... but *Road & Track* went on:

> 'The fact that small sports cars of this type are socially acceptable is also basic in the appeal. The competition image is important in this respect and, as a consequence, the Sprite and Spitfire both rank high because of their long-standing success in amateur sports car racing. The Sprite also enjoys additional prestige as it is a popular slalom or autocross competitor—and these are competitive events in which the young driver can participate.'

So far as individual judgement went, the students, Jay and Mike, decided on the Sprite:

> 'Excellent handling and straightforward mechanical specification. It would be hard to find a car that we could recommend more highly for the young driver who is interested in learning the good things there are to know about sports cars.'

Of the Datsun:

> 'Dollar for dollar, the Datsun offers more for the money than any other sports car. Yet for the audience for whom it should seem ideal, it's a bit fancier and a bit too expensive to hit the centre of the market target. It seems that a starker more nearly bare-bones model would increase its appeal with the younger market.'

Of the Fiat:

'The overall impression is that the Fiat tends to respond best to a light and delicate touch. It's a girl's car really.'

Of the Spitfire:

'We would fault the Spitfire on its swing-axle rear suspension but praise it for its driving position, performance, comfortable ride, pleasant appearance and engine accessibility.'

Autocar recorded similar performance figures to those of *Road & Track* when they tested a Midget on 9 February 1967, with a standing quarter mile of 19.7 seconds and fuel consumption of 30 mpg on average. They thoroughly liked their car (registered HOF 867D), commenting on its excellent gearbox (which, nevertheless, they wished had synchromesh on first gear). On other points they found that the ride and handling were 'in the best MG tradition', the brakes faultless, the new hood a great improvement, but the driving position cramped and the heater horrible. *Motor* were in complete agreement when they tested a Sprite, registered HOF 874D, on 9 September 1967, saying 'Fairly stiff and simple suspension gives a ride which is firm by modern standards, but which would have been considered unusually soft in the mark I Sprite era,' and obtaining 95 mph top speed with a standing quarter mile of 19.1 mph. *Cars and Car Conversions* improved this to 96 mph with a 12.2-second 0–60 in their test in August 1968, but John Bolster could manage only 94 mph for *Autosport* on 18 October 1968, with a Sprite registered LOC 258F.

The dumpy lines of the Arkley put off some people ... but proved to be a positive attraction to others. The saving in weight was so good that the Spridget underneath became far more responsive.

The uncompromising tail of the Arkley, notable for its lack of overhang.

Interior of the Arkley is pure Spridget, this car having been fitted with a leather-rimmed steering wheel.

Two models of Arkley have been marketed ... one with narrower wheels and the SS with the chunky, wide-rim wheels illustrated here.

You could be fooled into thinking that this really is a Lotus Eleven sports racing car from the 1950s, but in reality it is the Arkley's latter-day rival, the Westfield sports car, which can be based on any Spridget.

The Arkley SS

Several magazines published brief road impressions of what it was like to drive an Arkley SS, but only one—*Cars and Car Conversions*—really got involved with the vehicle: they built one! Technical assistant Jonathan Craymer's appetite for the project had been whetted by his experiences in a 1,275-cc model supplied for a test in September 1970 by the manufacturers, John Britten Garages. Craymer estimated that the Arkley Sprite's total weight was about 10 cwt and noted that the brakes and suspension worked much better as a result. The engine and gearbox were also far more responsive with less weight to propel, although the car sounded far noisier from the cockpit on the debit side. The very wide—7 inch—Goodyear tyres fitted were inflated to only 14 psi and endowed the SS (an S version was also marketed with narrower, 5.5-inch, rims), with truly phenomenal roadholding and a vastly improved ride, the steering remaining light because of the low weight. This car, registered 754 MOX, was fitted with a high 3.9:1 rear axle ratio that made high-speed cruising less frenetic and allowed it to return 30 mpg—but acceleration was still good, with an 11.1-second 0–60 time. Top speed suffered from the Arkley's blunt nose, however: it was only 90 mph.

Late 1275 cc Spridgets

Motor's road testers were unanimous in their enthusiasm for the Austin Healey Sprite when they tested one of the last made, registered VOP 436J, on 10 October 1970. They found the pulling power of the engine quite remarkable with acceleration up to 50 mph as good as they had ever experienced with a 1,275-cc Spridget, despite the use of the new higher, 3.9:1 axle ratio. The 0–60 time suffered marginally at 13.5 seconds, but they said they would have expected it to be about the same as before at 13 seconds when the car was fully run in. The standing quarter mile times were almost the same at 19.3 seconds as tested and 19.1 seconds earlier. So far as the fuel consumption was concerned, it was extraordinarily good at 36.3 mpg. The new across-the-tail exhaust system was also a lot more effective—some drivers even thought that it was now too quiet! But *Motor* said:

> 'With the hood down (it's very easy to lower and erect) 70 mph is a fairly relaxed cruising speed as mechanical noises are lost to the atmosphere and there's only wind roar around the screen pillars to disturb things—with the side windows up, there's not much buffeting either ...
>
> 'Although there are no changes to the suspension we thought the ride of this car much improved. Opinions on how best to label it varied from well-damped but bouncy to well-rounded but wooden. It's firm but certainly not jarring like that of early examples of the marque; over most surfaces it soaks up irregularities with ease. Round bumpy corners, though, the Sprite can be thrown off line, but it catches itself very quickly. On smooth corners the cornering powers are high; our Sprite was fitted with Michelin ZX radial tyres on the new and very handsome wheels. Why should anyone want to fit wire wheels which are heavier, weaker, and brutes to clean? Under power the car understeers mildly, though oversteer can be induced under power; on a semi-trailing throttle gentle oversteer sets in at the limit. The optional anti-roll bar was not fitted to our test car; this would promote more understeer and perhaps make the car even safer in inexperienced hands. Even without it you would have to be very foolish or unlucky to get into trouble ...
>
> 'All the switches, which are haphazardly strewn across the fascia, are within easy reach but you still have to get under the bonnet to regulate the heater hot water valve. The output is tremendous. Other recently added amenities are an ash tray on the transmission tunnel (at last BMC have realized that some sports car owners smoke ...)'

Motor obtained 95 mph from their Sprite and *Autocar* 94 when they tested a similar Midget, registered VOP 626J, for their issue of 4 February 1971, with virtually the same acceleration times. Their reactions were also similar to those of *Motor*, both magazines criticising the lack of synchromesh on first gear. *CAR* then compared the Midget *Autocar* had used with the latest Spitfire in June 1971. The Spitfire had by then received synchromesh on first gear and benefited enormously from suspension revisions that made its handling far less precarious. The Midget was still faster on acceleration, however, but felt decidedly cramped by comparison, having had far fewer attempts at modernisation over the years. *CAR* said: 'The Midget feels outdated now though the much more modern Spitfire should be good for a few years yet—especially with the boost of a 1500 engine.' *Motor Sport* had similar feelings about the Midget by the time they tested one, registered AOH 619K, in October 1972, but wound up deciding it was, after all, a thoroughly likeable car. Assistant editor Andrew Marriott wrote:

All you need to build a Westfield is a 'basket-case' Spridget and a kit, which comprises a Lotus-type space frame to replace the bodyshell, new suspension units, body panels and fuel tank. All the rest of the parts come straight from the Sprite ... with the author as an aspiring owner.

'For some years I have turned up my nose at the MG Midget—mainly because it can boast of no technological ingenuity whatsoever, the engine is frankly outdated by a decade and the performance is struggling to keep up with a number of saloons. When I have seen young men driving in shiny new MG Midgets I have thought 'what stick in the muds they must be'. For the same money the could have built themselves something like a Ginetta G15, rear-engined, overhead camshaft, performance with economy and superb handling. So, once in a while, the choke comes away in your hand, but to my mind the 1970s idea of a sports car is something in which you lie back in the cockpit, with finger steering, lightning brakes and some stylistic flair. Definitely not a solid old Midget which has hardly changed in 10 years.

'Having said all that I must say that I enjoyed driving the Midget far more than I ever expected. British Leyland have had a fair bit of experience at building the machines and they have certainly got them as right as they will ever be. For a start the car is now very much more comfortable than in the early days. However, the door catches on the inside are still extremely nasty and are ideal for breaking your finger nails, but otherwise the fixtures and fittings give no cause for complaint. I had the hood up and down a couple of times and found that on erecting the weather protection a quick application of the right foot in the appropriate place speeded up the proceedings!

'The performance was very much better than I had remembered. The A series engine may be old fashioned but it still does the job extremely well, if a little harshly. The gearbox proved an absolute delight to use being extremely quick apart from the lack of synchromesh on first, while the brakes stopped the car well ...

'My reacquaintance with the Midget allowed me to see this little car in a new light.'

The American rivals, *Car and Driver* and *Road & Track*, then staged the comparison test to end comparison tests—between the nine cars, including the Midget, allowed into the Sports Car Club of America's new showroom stock sports car class. Amazingly, both magazines published their test in April 1973 with only the venues, Ontario race track for *Car and Driver* and Riverside for *Road & Track*, as the only obvious differences. They even tried to equalise the cars for assessment by fitting them with the front-running SCCA tyre, Semperit's M401 radial of the maximum 165 section that could be used in the class that allowed virtually no other modifications.

It was hardly surprising that the Midget did not compare very well with the more expensive rivals; initially the SCCA had intended to confine the class—purely for cars built in 1972 and 1973—to ones costing less than $3,000, but this idea bit the dust because they could find only three: the Midget, the Spitfire and Volkswagen's Karmann Ghia. So they raised the ceiling to $4,000 and then made a special dispensation for Porsche's $4,600 914 because it was a popular marque with their members. So the Midget—highly-esteemed in the SCCA's H-production class at the time—wound up facing far more expensive rivals, Fiat's 124 Sport Spider, Opel's 1900GT, Triumph's GT6 and the MGB, besides the Spitfire, Porsche and Volkswagen, with only the VW showing less power. The Fiat came out on top of *Car and Driver's* lap times with the Midget sixth (ahead of the Spitfire and VW), and no allowance could be made in such a test for the fact that it was the cheapest car; *Road & Track*, in less track-like tests, relegated it to seventh!

Later 1,275 cc Spridgets featured British Leyland corporate slim-line bumpers.

Modified Late 1275 cc Spridgets

The Racing Car Show at Olympia in London and the prospect of supplementary advertising persuaded *Autocar* and *Motor* to test a representative range of British Leyland Special Tuning cars, including a very fast Midget, early in 1971, but *Motor* got the best out of the Midget, on 16 January.

The car, registered SOK 94H, had a 1,293-cc engine modified to full race specification, producing 97 bhp at 7,500 rpm. Twin 1.5-inch SU carburettors were fitted although other works listed Webers for even more top-end power. In this case, the engine pulled well from 2,500 rpm to give reasonably docile performance on the road. Chassis work on the Midget was confined to a front anti-roll bar and harder DS11 front brake pads: an impressive tribute to the car's basic ability to handle a lot of extra power. As *Motor* said after recording a 0–60 time of 9.2 seconds with a standing quarter mile in 17.2:

> 'Standing start times are impressive with take off accompanied by a lot of axle tramp. But by dropping the clutch at 6,000 rpm the revs stay above the 2,500–3,000 rpm "no-go" level and the car accelerates to 60 mph faster than the standard car to 50 mph; to 90 mph the time is halved from 45.7 sec to 22.9, which is a mere 0.3 sec longer than a Ford Capri 3000GT.
>
> 'With this balanced engine you ignore the red lines on the tachometer as Special Tuning set a limit at 7,800 rpm. So you pile on the revs until the tachometer hits the stop, hold it awhile then change—all rather unnerving until you get used to the idea. This makes the Midget's already well-chosen ratios even better for open road use as first is good for 40 mph (31 mph standard at 6,000), second 67 mph (52) and third 95 mph (73).
>
> 'The first time we tried to record a maximum speed we reached the tachometer-indicated rev limit before the end of our measured mile.

Motor found the pulling power of the 1275-cc engine quite remarkable and more than enough to make up for a new, higher, rear axle ratio.

Returning to base, we checked with the specification sheet, and noted the 7,800 limit. We tried again and this time recorded a staggering 112 mph lap, some 17 mph faster than standard, and again faster than a Capri 3000 GT.'

Autocar found the same Midget to be the most impressive of the cars tested, although they were not all to the same state of tune. *Autocar* explained:

'On the open road, the performance was nothing short of exhilarating, although again the noise level was high enough to become wearing after an hour or so of really hard driving. For this sort of driving we felt it fairest to adhere to a 7,000 rev limit, giving a use speed bonus in each of the lower gears compared with what the standard car can achieve at its red line of 6,400 rpm ...

'Even the basic Spridget is a power-handling car. The extra stability and cornering power with the throttle open is very obvious. In the Special Tuning Midget, it is more obvious still; the chosen line can be altered to a considerable extent simply by shifting the right foot a little ...

'The test car proved very convincingly that the Spridget takes well even to extreme tuning of this kind. The conversion greatly enhanced the sporting character of the car without any serious snags arising; even the fuel consumption stayed within very reasonable bounds (at 26 mpg overall).'

One of the delights of a Sprite, as *Motor* discovered with their 1970 model (of the type illustrated) was how well it handled in adverse conditions.

Cars and Car Conversions then tested a Midget with similar performance at a similar price, just £200 more than that of a standard car. But the way in which the extra performance was achieved was extraordinary: the Midget was fitted with a Ford Mexico engine and gearbox, that also gave it a synchronised first gear. These converted cars, called the Atlantis, by Car Preparations in Bedford, were intended only to use new Midgets as a basis. The cost was kept low by the profit made on selling the new cars. In any case, they were only feasible on 1,275 cc Spridgets without resorting to floorpan surgery. The 1,600 cc four-cylinder in-line Ford engine produced 86 bhp in standard form with absolutely

John Sprinzel continued to modify Spridgets after the Frogeye went out of production, with this example featuring much of the equipment that was to be used on the Special Tuning cars, including the wide-rimmed Minilite magnesium wheels.

no displays of temperament and the gearbox was recognised as being superb; fortunately it also had the right ratios! The test car, registered OVV 433J, was also fitted with the optional 3.727:1 rear axle ratio for more relaxed cruising, a rise in gearing with which the Ford engine was well able to cope. It was worth noting that other tuners at the time had been fitting Ford rear axles to Midgets for competition because they had stronger half shafts and a more readily-available limited-slip differential. The only disadvantages were that the slightly wider track of the Ford Escort (or Mexico) axle needed wheelarch modifications and the range of final drives for it were rather more limited. Despite natural loyalties to MG, assistant editor Clive Richardson, a former Abingdon employee, was very enthusiastic about the Ford conversions. He wrote:

'The Atlantis surprises in every way: in price, performance, handling and practicability. It is far from being a "special": it represents the ideal marriage of diverse products and the only pity is that British Leyland do not have a similar engine with which they could transform the car in production.'

With similar suspension and braking modifications to those of the Special Tuning Midget, the Atlantis—the bodyshell of which needed only minimal modification to accept the Ford power train—was nearly as fast: its maximum speed of 106 mph, with a 10.3-second 0–60 could be accounted for by an increase in overall weight of about 1 cwt. Against that could be balanced the complete lack of temperament and extra noise, much improved torque, and undoubted durability of its relatively understressed engine. Fuel consumption was about the same and the Atlantis even had a 10 gallon tank for a superior range.

A Weber carburettor and alloy rocker cover were typical of the equipment fitted to Special Tuning cars.

The Rubber-Bumpered Midgets

While the Triumph 1500 engine fitted to the rubber-bumpered Midgets offered more torque than before, it had nowhere near so much as the 92 lb/ft of the Ford unit—but it still made a world of difference to British Leyland's revised car. *Autocar* extracted a maximum speed of 101 mph from their Midget, registered TOF 553N, by running 100 rpm into the red on the rev counter's 6,000 limit. With this evidence of undergearing, they pointed out that a higher final drive would also give it better maximum speeds in the intermediate ratios as well as superior fuel economy—28 mpg on the test car. They found the gap between second gear, with a 47-mph maximum, and third, just short of 70, particularly noticeable although it was disguised by the improved torque. The extra pulling power assisted by the lower gearing more than compensated for the increased weight, however. Standing start acceleration figures were a lot better, with a 12.3-second 0–60 and a 35.3-second 0–90; 16 seconds faster than a 1275 Spridget. The standing quarter mile was also down to 18.5 sec.

Of the handling, it was a case of love or hate. *Autocar* said:

> 'Part of the trouble lies in the fact that the Midget, like the MGB, has been given increased ride height at the back to compensate for the greater weight of its "5 mph" bumpers and associated structure. As a result, roll stiffness at the back end has been reduced and there is much more tendency to oversteer. This is despite the heavier engine which means the front wheels bear a greater part of the total weight …
>
> 'It is not evident at first, for in gentle driving the Midget stays very close to neutral. When driven harder into a corner, if the driver holds the

Other modifications were less ambitious, confined in this case to such items as less-restrictive air cleaners.

wheel and accelerator steady, the tail will come out steadily until some of the lock has to be paid off before the car gets too sideways. In itself it is no bad thing, for it enables the Midget to be driven in distinctly sporting fashion by someone who knows what he is doing. At the same time it holds the seeds of danger for anyone less clever.

'The real snag to the Midget's handling in 1500 form lies in its sensitivity to the throttle. Given the previous situation where the car has been wound hard into a long, tight bend, any sudden release of the accelerator will bring the tail out very smartly, calling for opposite lock to pin it down. Again, this situation is beloved of some drivers but it means that the Midget is much less predictable, and certainly calls for more skill, than many small saloons of equal performance and cornering ability. The drawback is compounded by limited roadholding, which can leave the car well-balanced fore and aft, but skittering sideways onto a wider line than desired … it is difficult to avoid the conclusion that the 1500 is somewhat undertyred. In the wet, the roadholding is considerably reduced and the Midget tends to skate around on smooth-surfaced corners. In this case, however, it is much more forgiving and the quick steering really comes into its own.'

Autocar then raised points such as the cramped interior and economy fittings that had rankled with the later Spridgets, before *Motor* compared the latest Midget, once more, with the equivalent Spitfire—which shared the same power train, of course—on 24 May 1975.

Despite the reduction in power caused by the installation difficulties in the Midget (*Motor*'s car was registered TOF 557N), performance of the two models was almost the same. The Spitfire scored with its optional overdrive on fuel economy and on finish with a comfort pack, although the price was much higher as a result. But the Midget's steering was still felt far better despite using the same rack and the handling was far more entertaining.

John Bolster was in restrained agreement when he tested a 1500 Midget for *Autosport* on 13 July 1978, but pointed out that seeing as it outperformed far more modern competition such as the Fiat X1/9, it still took a lot of beating if you appreciated fresh air. In his judgement, it was still an enormously enjoyable little car.

Road & Track also found the Midget still had an endearing appeal, despite problems with the brake, and a top speed reduced by emission equipment to 86 mph. They said when they tested one in May 1976:

'There is still plenty of noise, mechanical and wind, and that means the car seems to be going fast at almost any speed. With the top down, and this is still not a simple task although it has been improved, the speed sensation goes up dramatically. And perhaps this is what the car is all about. All the elements are there for the young enthusiast: wind in the face, lots of gear changing, and a plethora of sports car noises. Power becomes rather secondary in this type of driving and responsiveness is of primary importance. The Midget also meets many of the other rudimentary requirements of a sports car: it has a proud name earned in road racing competition, there is an awareness of things mechanical going on all about you from the note of the exhaust to the whine of the gearbox, and there are gauges for monitoring vital functions rather than warning lights. All of these qualities come together in making a sports car something that demands to be driven with verve and expertise.

'All in all, despite its outdated design and time-worn engineering, the Midget still provides that most important quality: it's fun to drive in the sports car tradition.'

Road testers had mixed feelings about the handling of 'rubber-bumper' Midgets but it is possible to drive one at the limit in a tidy manner, as this one in production sports car racing shows.

Most of the writers on the staff of *Car and Driver* had a go at writing the epitaph to the Midget in the guise of a road test in August 1979 when they heard it was going out of production, but sports editor Larry Griffin won hands down with this statement:

'Decades ago, when God instructed the British about sports cars, He laid down an absolute formula, to be followed, no matter what, with a stiff upper lip. The design staff at MG has, by God, the stiffest upper lip this side of Alice McDaniels. But that's another story. MG's lack of progress is of no importance here, because there is no modern *rationale* for a little dart game like the Midget. It's not supposed to make sense and never has. This shrunken buzz bomb has got some real *whoopeee!* ballistics. It converts every tight corner, small crosswind, and big truck into a madcap change of direction, like an atomic mouse in an elephant compound. It has Woody Allen's vaguely wild-eyed approach to life, but for following Diane Keaton to the ends of the earth, you'll want something else, because this teensy car gets familiar with every corner of your body, and the seats are squishy. Every decisive move in the cockpit makes something dramatic happen. If you haven't driven an X1/9, maybe you can love a Midget. If you can fit. Maybe.'

VI

The Spridget in Competition

It is hardly surprising that Spridgets have enjoyed a successful competition career and continue to do so; they have such inherently good handling and superb steering, and their sheer strength and low cost make them ideal mounts for the impecunious. But what has always been surprising is the way in which they have been made to perform in the higher echelons against far more specialised and expensive machinery. This was partly due to the extraordinary degree in which the basic A-series engine was developed for other purposes. Initially, a good deal of extra power was extracted by independent tuners, notably Harry Weslake, who had been responsible for the cylinder head in the first place. The first cars to take advantage of higher-powered A-series engines were sports machines such as those made by Lotus, and the A35 in saloon car racing. The Morris Minor was never in the same league because it had a problem with axle tramp, although odd works' examples competed in rallies. But no sooner had Sprite production got into full swing, and its first international rally success been recorded, than the revolutionary Mini was introduced. This extraordinary little 'tin box' used basically the same mechanical components and proved to be even easier to handle with a wheel at each corner and follow-my-leader front-wheel drive. It soon became BMC's front-line rally car with the far more powerful Austin Healey 3000. Although the Mini had only about the same power-to-weight ratio as the Sprite, it had a big advantage in that it could compete in classes for saloon cars, which often had an advantageous handicap over those for GT cars. The Sprite, as a sports car, could only just about qualify as a GT car. Both the Sprite and the Mini were helped by a tremendous surge of interest in Formula Junior, a new form of racing started as a cheap method of training up-and-coming racing drivers. Like almost every other formula with such aspirations, it soon became very expensive as major manufacturers fought to scoop publicity with more and more highly-developed cars. It was for this reason that a truly exceptional amount of power was extracted from the A-series engine, to the ultimate benefit of the Spridget and Mini.

Numerous top names were involved with the Spridget at one time or another, but only two, John Sprinzel, and the Healey Motor Company, with their vested interest in development, stuck with the Spridget throughout its international racing career. Most other people went on to far more adventurous machines!

Sprinzel originally became involved with the Spridget through rallying and racing, first an A30 and then an A35. He enjoyed so much the success that he left his family printing works and started the Speedwell tuning business with George Hulbert and company, before quitting to run the Healeys' venture in this line. This did not enjoy so much success as Speedwell, partly because it stuck to Austin Healeys, whereas private concerns could engage themselves with any sort of car, particularly the Mini. As a result, Sprinzel then went on to run his own tuning business, Sprinzel Racing. During his A35 days he had become a BMC works driver, and when the Sprite was only six weeks old, he took one registered PMO 200 to a magnificent class win in the 1958 Alpine Rally. This car had been prepared with the rest of the BMC rally team at Abingdon, the contemporary Big Healey rally team cars bearing the numbers PMO 201, 202 and 203. Rally enthusiasts are great number plate spotters, and Sprinzel was a particularly gifted publicist, so he retained the number plate PMO 200 for all his future Spridgets. He was supported in the 1958 Alpine by journalist Tommy Wisdom—who was also, in effect, a Healey Motor Company works driver—in second place in the 1000 cc class and BMC works team member Ray Brookes third in another Frogeye.

Sprinzel was to say later in the now-defunct *Collector's Car* magazine of the Alpine Rally in those days:

'It was originally intended as a pure test of the production car, but became faster, more demanding and of a greater reputation each year. The organisers—those incredible enthusiasts from Marseilles—would search out and find tougher and twistier passes to add to the favourites, and as crews became more professional—and faster—so the target times for each section were cut, and generally the fastest recorded time in each class

Deep in the heart of the Speedwell tuning concern ... work progresses on customers' cars: a Lotus Elite on the ramp, and an MGA behind it, with their Lotus Seven series one demonstrator in the foreground and on the right, on its trailer. The Speedwell Sprite record car is complete with standard doors, still visible beneath the special body panels.

became the "bogey" for the following year. For those such as I, battling it out with little Sprites, certain tests were set with a need to keep within 10 per cent of the speed of the fastest cars, which tended to limit the awards to the more powerful cars. But this calculation only included finishers, so the fragile speedsters who failed to arrive fortunately didn't worry us unduly.'

For political and economic reasons, there were not many French entries in the Alpine that year, which helped the Sprites, but these rivals returned with a vengeance later and that victory was never repeated. The chief opposition was usually made up of Abarths which bore far less resemblance to the Fiats on which they were based than the rally Sprites to standard models. In fact, it was amazing how little was changed in the early competition Sprites, which proved to be one of their great strengths in rallies like the incredible Liege-Rome-Liege. Sprinzel remembered in *Collector's Car*:

'Probably the best-loved and certainly the toughest annual event in post-war motor sport, the Liege didn't start from Liege, and hadn't been to Rome since the early 1950s. Instead, the 5,000-kilometer route started from the town centre of Spa, hurried to the majestic passes of the Dolomites and into Yugoslavia for the roughest tracks in Europe—and in later years ran to Sophia in Bulgaria for a brief pause before returning to tackle more of the same challenging tracks. The final night's fling, the fourth in 90 hours of virtually non-stop racing, took in a collection of the classic mountain passes of South Eastern France, before the exhausted survivors returned north to Spa for a triumphant victory convoy. The dirty

Sprites as they used to compete ... Luca Grandori takes the chicane in his Frogeye, believed to be one of the ex-Warwick rally cars, in the 1982 Donington Historic Weekend's GT race.

dozen, tired and shattered survivors, were hailed with garlands as they pushed through the crowd-lined streets into the heart of Liege.

'No words can describe how tough the unique challenge of the Marathon de la Route had become ... but just ask any of the drivers who took part and see their eyes glaze over with the reverence of an event they seemed to adore the tougher and harder it became.

'Nowhere in the regulations was there ever a mention of the world rally—except to state that the event qualified for the European Rally Championship—yet the listed average speeds to be attained between control points were scheduled at a modest 30 mph. Monsieur Garot and his enthusiastic organisers ensured that this lip-service to police requirements would still provide a suitable challenge by also listing the times—on another page—during which these control points would be open to each competitor. True, if you kept to these averages, you would not be penalised, nor would you find more than the first two or three controls open for you, and you would return to the finish about a day and a half after the rally had ended. By this simple method you were obliged to travel virtually flat out for nearly four days and nights in order to arrive at each control while it was still open for you. The winner would lose penalties in hours rather than minutes when the second timing was actually applied, and generally the leaderboard would emerge on the road to avoid any confusion for spectators.

'Police speed checks were secret—but Monsieur Garot held their location aloft, waving a scrap of paper ...

'Ferrari, Porsche, Mercedes, Healey, Alpine, Alfa, Volvo, SAAB, MG and Triumph joined with the specially-built one-offs and modified production saloons all assembled to a simple formula which only specified that a car must comply with traffic regulations and should have four wheels—though as far as I can recall, no official from this most sporting of motor clubs was ever seen to count them.'

Peter Preston campaigns his Frogeye in the spirit of the old marque racing so popular at the time the model was introduced, in the British Thoroughbred modified championship. He is pictured here finishing third in his class with his 1,275-cc-engined car at Brands Hatch in October 1982.

Preston leads the Aston Martin DB4s of David Furzeland (right) and Alistair Sinclair (left) before having to retire to the Aston Martin Owners' Club Bovis Trophy race at Brands Hatch in May 1983.

No protests were accepted either, and the competitors were left to get on with what amounted to the world's last great road race over the most appalling surfaces the organisers could find. Dust, punctures, other traffic (not necessarily motorised), and crashes, were frequent. Rarely did more than a handful of the 100 or so entrants finish. It was in this atmosphere that Sprinzel and his Sprite did so well. He won his class with eighth place overall in 1959 after having been eliminated with a broken stub axle in 1958. Then in 1960 he won his class—with third place overall! Pat Moss and Tommy Wisdom's daughter, Ann, won the event outright that year with a Big Healey and put the Austin Healey name on an unparalleled high spot.

Sprinzel switched to a SAAB with European Rally Championship leader Eric Carlsson for the 1959 RAC Rally—when appalling November weather prevented all bar 16 crews from reaching one control at Braemar. However, despite having to stop to repair a broken throttle cable four times, Tommy Gold won his class with a Sprite and took second place overall to a works Ford Zephyr. Sprinzel was back in a Sprite with journalist Dickie Bensted-Smith to repeat the trick in the 1960 RAC Rally before this event became one of special stages on forest tracks that made it far more suitable for cars such as the Mini. Sprinzel had also managed third place in his class in the 1959 Monte Carlo Rally ... but enthusiasts chiefly thought of the Sprite as a clubman's rally car rather

Preston lines up again for the All-Comers' Handicap race at the 1983 Donington weekend ... as an illustration of some of the variety of events run in Britain for historic sports cars such as the Sprite.

than as the ideal machine for internationals. When rallies were made up chiefly of long road sections between gymkhana-like driving tests, the Sprite was in its element. It could safely keep up a decent average on the road, and then with hood down for maximum visibility, make mincemeat of bigger cars in driving tests thanks to its nimble handling and steering. Despite Sprinzel's epic runs in the Liege, the Sprite was at a positive disadvantage when the going got really rough and slippery on forest tracks.

These efforts provided the Sprite with a lot of good publicity, but somehow it fell down in this context on the track. There was no hope of an overall win in major events against far more powerful and specialised cars, so the BMC competitions department at Abingdon could not put aside potentially more rewarding work to spend much time on development. In fact, they only prepared Sprites for rallies because they were forced to by BMC's sales department. As a result the Sprite ran alongside such as the Morris Minor 1000 and Austin A40 as some sort of novelty compared to a big Healey, and soon, the Mini. But because it performed so well, more by luck than judgement on the part of the competitions department, in near-standard form, it achieved a good quantity of publicity.

This lack of interest in a car that was unlikely to win the top awards left the field open to the Healeys in the classic races they loved so much. They used their BMC development contract to good effect with a series of prototypes that performed in the most creditable manner. Even with Formula Junior engines in their eventual form, however, they needed a bit of extra help, so they were given highly-streamlined bodies. This gave many onlookers the impression that they were far more highly-modified than was really the case. Other manufacturers got away with such changes and still scooped a great deal of publicity for their basic car, but not the Healeys.

This was almost undoubtedly because of record-breaking cars built by the MG factory—as opposed to the BMC competitions department, which shared part of the same factory complex at Abingdon. In the past, MG had benefited tremendously from publicity gained by these exotic specials, often with a much-modified engine as the only link with production cars. These machines shattered all sorts of records, many of them rather obscure. They invariably featured highly-streamlined bodywork that made them look nothing like the car they were supposed to be. The whole idea was a hangover from the time when today's record-breaker was tomorrow's production car, but had developed to such a degree by the time the Sprite was introduced that nobody was fooled any more, no matter how hard the publicity men tried. Unfortunately, this also gave rise to the suspicion that the Healey's Sprites with non-standard bodywork had only a tenuous relationship to production vehicles. It was a great pity that the publicity department could never quite get over the message that they were, in fact, quite like normal cars in most respects—while the Healeys remained convinced that eventually the public would see the light as they saw it.

They even tried to convince BMC that they should run a special-bodied Sprite with a Coventry Climax engine like that used in the rival Lotus Elite—but BMC refused to back this idea because they could no longer claim then that it was simply a slightly-modified production car. Ironically, virtually all 'production' cars in competition today are far more highly-modified than anything the Healeys produced at Warwick—and still scoop all available publicity because they look like the cars on which they are based.

However, when Sprites of standard appearance were raced, notably at Sebring, the publicity was excellent. Four were built at Warwick for the 1959 12-hour race, with disc brakes to cope with this notorious American circuit's tight corners. Geoffrey Healey remembers them as having engines of only 57 bhp tuned more for reliability than outright power, but also says they were capable of 98 mph. So it would appear that the 57 horses were uncommonly strong ones! Sprinzel's experiences with stub axles in the 1958 Liege rally had also led to stronger parts being developed for these cars, to the ultimate benefit of production models. These cars, which were of very similar specification to road test machines prepared by the Healeys, took the first three places in their class, with the front runner in 15th place overall driven by Hugh Sutherland and Phil Stiles.

At the same time, Wisdom managed to get BMC's backing to run a similar car in the Targa Florio two months later, in company with French journalist Bernard Cahier. Despite the use of disc brakes on the Sebring cars, this machine—again of standard appearance—had only the larger, 8-inch drum front brakes from the Austin A40 as an aid to stopping power. Despite problems with a split fuel tank and the Sprite's old bogey, a broken throttle cable, it took sixth place in its class and 17th overall. But although the Targa has now been recognised as one of the greatest road races even, it seemed far away to the average British or American enthusiast at that time and this highly-creditable showing had little effect on sales. It would be five years before the Healeys returned to Sicily and by then they were into Sprites of a completely different appearance.

They had been inspired partly by MG's success with a record-breaking 'Sprite', codenamed EX219 because it was an Abingdon project. This was, in reality, an earlier MG record-breaker, EX179, that had nothing to do with anything Austin Healey! It consisted of an early experimental MGA chassis fitted with special bodywork that formed part of Syd Enever's studies while designing the MGA. This car, originally constructed in 1954 around a 1951 chassis, had already taken 33 international records with a variety of MG engines

John Dalton takes the Falcon-bodied Sprite shared with John Colgate to a win in the 1100-cc sports car class, with 16th place overall, at Le Mans in 1960 despite suffering from an early A-series malady of pumping oil through the rear main oil seal as the bearings wore at high revs.

before it was fitted with a 950-cc A-series engine using all the current competition parts. MG, and Enever in particular, were experts at the art of supercharging to take records, so they fitted a low-pressure Shorrock unit of the type that Healeys were subsequently to offer on their supercharged Sprites. The supercharger's pressure could be varied by altering the size of its driving pulleys. For 12-hour records it ran in 70 bhp form with a 2.88:1 rear axle ratio, rising to 98 bhp with a higher-compression head for a one-hour blind. As the existing holder of the international class G 12-hour record, Wisdom drove the car with North American BMC team men Gus Ehrman and Ed Leavens. EX219 had no trouble at all in smashing fifteen records at Utah in September 1959 with a top average speed of 146.95 mph. The previous one-hour record had been held by a Lotus-Climax, so the Healeys promptly put aside their Climax Sprite and resolved that that was the way to go in competition ... with a supercharged engine where possible and certainly with streamlined bodywork.

At the same time, Enever produced another record-breaker, an MG codenamed EX181, based on a far-more advanced, but redundant spaceframe, chassis he had hoped would form the basis of an MG road racer in 1957. The body on this car was also far more streamlined and became his inspiration behind the MGB, and indirectly, the revised front end for the first Spridget.

Sprinzel, at Speedwell, was alert to any publicity that could be gleaned from these record-breaking efforts and before he moved to Healeys, instigated a Speedwell record car to show off their conversions. This was built up with a Costin-designed body along similar lines to that of EX219, but far higher because it was based on a standard Sprite floorpan scuttle and running gear as used in GT racing. Without the benefit of a supercharger and a large factory budget, this car achieved 132.2 mph along the Liege-Antwerp motorway in Graham Hill's hands in April 1960 to demolish Belgium's class G records! But

There's snow on the windscreen as John Sprinzel's service crew change a wheel at the Rest and Be Thankful hillclimb in Scotland on the 1960 RAC Rally. He was to lose two marks on this rock-strewn stage—enough to relegate him to second place behind the overall winner, Eric Carlsson, in a Saab which had far more ground clearance.

After that, Sebring Sprites stuck chiefly to the track, with this semi-works example being campaigned under the Unipart banner throughout the 1983 season on British tracks.

because it was far nearer, in reality, to a basic Sprite, the publicity did Speedwell a lot of good. At the same time, Reg Venner-Pack, who had become a partner at Speedwell in place of Sprinzel—by then departed to Healeys—took along his Speedwell Sprite GT racer to record 110.9 mph and give David Phipps the chance of the ultimate road test for *Sports Cars Illustrated*.

Meanwhile, the Healeys cast around for a suitable body to use on the Sprite in the 1960 season. Ford and Austin Seven specials at that time were being fitted with rather pretty open Falcon bodies of similar appearance to a D type Jaguar but made from glass fibre like the pioneering Lotus Elite. This body also attracted Colin Chapman, who adapted one for a prototype that eventually became the Lotus Elan!

There were two races at Sebring that year, one of four hours' duration for GT cars using homologated equipment and the 12-hour in which prototypes could run. So the Targa Florio Sprite was prepared for the shorter race with disc brakes, wire wheels and more power extracted by Harry Weslake, while the 1959 road test car, registered 5983 AC, was prepared for the big race with a Falcon shell. This car was considerably lighter than normal as a result and also used disc brakes on all four wheels. Both cars suffered from cylinder head problems that resulted in the casting being made thicker and more rigid at the joint face. The four-hour car was driven by Stirling Moss—at that time the world's top sports car driver (and the best never to win a world championship). But despite Stirling's efforts, and possibly because of a patched-up cylinder head, the standard-looking Sprite was narrowly beaten by a highly-sophisticated twin cam Fiat Abarth. Moss was driving a Maserati in the big race, so Sprinzel took over the Falcon-bodied car with John Lumkin. Despite losing a lot of time with a gasket change, they struggled in to finish 41st—and had the consolation of winning their class as its only finisher.

This machine was then taken to Le Mans, where, at the organisers' insistance, it had to be fitted with a full-size windscreen. The scuttle height had

Sprinzel was as keen as ever to continue racing his creations. He is pictured here leading a team of Sebring Sprites to a six-lap victory in the classic of British club racing, the 750MC's Six-Hour Relay, at Silverstone in 1961. It was a glorious day for the marque Austin Healey, with a works stable of 3000s second. For the record, the Sebring Sprite drivers with Sprinzel were Chris Williams, Douglas Wilson-Spratt, David Siegle-Morris, Peter Jackson, and Ian Walker.

already been lowered to that of the steering column itself, so the new screen not only looked awful, but presented a lot of drag. The bodywork behind the screen had to be modified as well to comply with regulations over space for theoretical luggage and the result was such a hotch potch that the Healeys resolved to have their streamlined bodies constructed as one unit from scratch in future rather than getting involved in tacking bits and pieces on somebody else's creation.

The insistance by the organisers at Le Mans on a full screen, luggage space and so on, was all part of a laudable attempt to force cars into retaining some resemblance to those that ran on the road—but they were eventually defeated by a combination of drivers who couldn't see properly through awkward, dirt-caked, screens and crowds who were attracted chiefly by the sheer speed and spectacle of all-out racing cars with highly-streamlined bodies. As a result, Le Mans kept its crowds but lost much of its importance in relation to the sales of normal cars.

Sprinzel had been injured a month earlier in the Acropolis Rally, so Austin Healey club racer John Dalton joined John Colgate to take this Formula Junior-engined Sprite to 16th place overall and a win in the 1,000 cc class.

Despite his connections with the BMC works rally team, the Healey works racing team, and their tuning business, Sprinzel was officially a private entrant. He did enjoy a good deal of independence, though, and was able to prove that enough Sprites had been fitted with Speedwell-style bodywork to qualify them for international racing in 1961—promptly calling them 'Sebring' Sprites despite the name having been registered by Healeys! As a result, an amazing variety of Sprites appeared at Sebring in 1961 with three distinct body styles. There was the standard shape (moulded in glass fibre to save weight), a revised version of the Falcon shape, and the Sprinzel Sebring Sprites, which looked just like Costin's original design. They all featured standard-shaped air intakes, however, in the vain hope that nobody would be confused as to the cars' origins!

The Sprinzel Sprites had been homologated, so they ran in both the 4- and

It was during 1961 that Wilson-Spratt produced the first examples of what looked like his own version of a Sebring Sprite, the WSM. It might have shared similar bodylines, but beneath the skin it was considerably different with its most notable feature being a space frame. This example is being raced by Richard Higgins in the Seldon Classic Sports Car Championship round at Donington in April 1982.

The Ecurie Ecosse Sprite that raced at Le Mans in 1961 had a long-nose bonnet of similar profile to that of the works car, and with a hardtop along the same lines—but the rest of the panels were the same as those of a normal Sprite. It is seen here leading two Ferraris before crashing in the third hour.

12-hour events; the 'standard' Sprites built at Warwick, ran in the 4-hour and the 'Falcon'—or 'Le Mans'—Sprites in the 12-hour race.

The 'standard' Sprites got the most publicity because they looked more like ordinary cars—a situation that was not lost on BMC. And then two of them, driven by Walt Hansgen and Bruce McLaren, proceeded to finish in front of the Sebrings—despite Sprinzel having persuaded Stirling and Pat Moss to drive them. They were all beaten by two Abarths, but BMC's salesmen started to wonder about the wisdom of changing the bodyshape so much. In the 12-hour race, the Le Mans Sprites, driven by Joe Buzzetta and Glen Carlson, and Leavens and Colgate, took 15th and 25th places, with Sprinzel and Paul Hawkins 37th. On the whole, however, the Sprites had done so well that it was definitely worth continuing in long-distance racing.

By 1961, the Jaguar D types that had won three times in succession at Le Mans were no longer competitive in three-litre form and their chief exponent, the Scottish national racing team Ecurie Ecosse, were searching for new machinery. They thought they would stand a good chance of overall victory with a Cooper Monaco—a thinly-disguised Grand Prix car—but realised that it was fragile and wanted something thoroughly reliable to back it up and make sure they won enough money to pay for the exercise. They were also very patriotic and opted for a Sprite as the best British contender for the highly-rewarding index of efficiency. So, with some extra finance, the Healeys rebuilt the 1960 car in coupé form along the lines of the Climax Sprite, with similar aluminium panels for the Hansgen Sebring car, which would be used by the Ecurie Ecosse. Their integral hard top not only offered superior streamlining, but made the car a good deal more comfortable—and less tiring—for the drivers. Its lines were

The works car used at Le Mans in 1961 had a smaller air intake than normal and the Super Sprite's swage line along the sides. It also featured the spare wheel hatch that the Healeys would have liked to have seen on the Frogeye, and small vertical catches to open the doors from the outside.

similar to those of a special-bodied MGA developed by Enever, which had raced neck and neck with the Sprite the year before. The rest of the Sprite followed the general lines of the design they would have liked to have introduced originally with retractable headlights. In fact, they still hoped that BMC would accept it, perhaps in open form, as a Super Sprite. This car also had what had become almost a Healey trademark on the 3000—a swage line running the length of the body.

Both cars were fitted with the latest line in BMC 994-cc Formula Junior engines as used in the Cooper works team. In the event, the works car, driven by

Despite the increasing severity of the forest tracks in the RAC Rally, Derek Astle and Peter Roberts took tenth place in their MG Midget in 1961 ... Peter Riley and Mike Hughes are pictured heading for their Monte Carlo Rally class win two months later.

Stirling Moss insisted on his Sprite being fitted with longer than usual bonnet straps for the 1962 Sebring race. He said that it might save time in the pits ... and the car retained this feature when Christabel Carlisle took it to 11th place in the next year's Nurburgring 1000-kilometre race.

Colgate and Hawkins, succumbed to a holed piston after the Ecurie Ecosse's new driver, Bill McKay, had crashed at White House.

Meanwhile, less professional drivers had been having a wonderful time in every conceivable form of club competition with their Sprites. One in particular, garage proprietor Douglas Wilson-Spratt, had even won a rally with a Frogeye within a week of its introduction and continued to have quite a reasonable amount of success at international level. He was a keen advocate of the use of roll-over bars, having survived a nasty experience years before. Wilson-Spratt was also an instinctive engineer who realised that such bars could be used for the dual purpose of strengthening the basic structure of the car.

One of the main problems with lightening the Sprite's bodywork was in losing some of its rigidity, although this was an essential course to follow if private cars were to remain at all competitive in works entries. This led Wilson-Spratt to build up a new Sprite for the 1962 Monte Carlo Rally with a roll cage so stiff that he felt quite happy to use a glass fibre rear end with a luggage boot lid in addition to having a Sebring-style bonnet of the same material. He used aluminium for its hardtop, however, as he was still wary of what might happen if he overturned again!

Wilson-Spratt was much encouraged by being able to take seventh place in his class behind such stars as Sprinzel and Christabel Carlisle, who could manage only fourth in a works car. As a result, he continued making special-bodied Sprites—and MGBs—for years, calling them WSMs after Wilson-Spratt Motors.

The first WSMs were built in 1961 for track use. They were generally made up of a Spridget floorpan with rear bulkhead and scuttle removed and the strength replaced by a tubular spaceframe. They were then clothed in a very pretty windcheating aluminium body even nearer to the lines of a Lotus Elite than those of the Sebring Sprites. These lovely little cars were also as much as 3 cwt lighter than a standard Spridget and eventually gave rise to some truly extraordinary machines in club racing.

Meanwhile the first Spridgets had been introduced and BMC were anxious to publicise the new shape although it offered more wind resistance than the Frogeye and certainly the Sebrings.

So they ran off several sets of new-shape light weight panels in aluminium and four cars were built at Warwick for Sebring in 1962. The Healeys also built a special-bodied car for the 12-hour race. Ten Sprites lined up against 13 Abarths in the supporting event, which had been cut to three hours, and it really looked as though a British car would win at last as Stirling Moss led until 15 minutes from the end—but then he had to stop unexpectedly for fuel, letting McLaren and Hansgen through to win in Abarths.

Film star Steve McQueen, a long-time competitor in SCCA club racing, put in a steady drive for 9th place in one of the Warwick Sprites before having the misfortune to break a connecting rod in the 12-hour car. This had been fitted with a special 100 bhp 1,098 cc engine with a stroke of only 62.25 mm as opposed to the rather weak 1098 engine that was about to go into production.

The Healeys did not want to become involved in the hurly burly of domestic racing because competitions almost every week would have left them with hardly any time for potentially more rewarding development—which was precisely why the BMC competitions department were also loath to involve themselves with too many cars. So when an enthusiastic MG dealer and former racing driver, Dick Jacobs, approached his old mentors at Abingdon, Thornley and Enever, with a suggestion that he might run a team of Midgets in GT racing, he was well received.

He, too, realised that the rather square-fronted Midget needed some aerodynamic help if it was to be successful in top flight competition, and suggested that it might be possible to follow to advantage the lines of the recently-introduced Aston Martin DB4. As long-time fans of this most British of exotic cars, Thornley and Enever thought deeply about such a project.

Thornley, in particular, was keen to increase the scope of his range with a two plus two hardtop car, and realised that he could raise enthusiasm internally with a successful competition model. Enever worked wonders by adapting the nose shape of EX181 and the Aston's long sweeping fastback lines to the Midget's shell without altering its appearance dramatically. In fact, the new cars still looked very much like Midgets although they were of far lower drag. Abingdon's efforts in this direction were eventually rewarded when the MGB GT went into production. The smaller Sprite was not a practical proposition in this context.

Three of these special Midgets were built, two for Jacobs and one for John

Sebring Sprites continued to compete all over the world, with Joel Naive pictured here at Laguna Seca in the American circuit's 1980 historic race weekend.

Milne to race in Scotland, and it was one of Jacobs' that was eventually tested by Phillips for *Autosport*. Jacobs engaged BMC regulars Andrew Hedges and Alan Foster as his drivers.

In their first season these cars were raced with considerable success in both domestic and international events, using 995 cc Formula Junior-based engines like those fitted to Sprites for Le Mans. The chief difference was that they had heavier pistons for extra strength. In this form, the Midgets proved outstandingly reliable and on occasions competitive against far more expensive and larger-capacity cars such as Porsche 356s. But the most important part of their season was *Autosport*'s domestic GT series, which had been created for series production cars when sports racing machinery became too specialised. The grand finale of this series was a three-hour race at Snetterton which the Midgets celebrated by taking first and second places in their class. The chief opposition in this case came from Turners and Marcos.

During the close season, the 1,098-cc engine qualified for this form of GT racing, so the Midgets were prepared at Abingdon with 1,139-cc units—this capacity representing the maximum permissable overbore. They now faced Lotus Elites in the 1,300 class and one occasion the Healeys were persuaded to enter the British Grand Prix's supporting event at Silverstone. Their car was the alloy-bodied one that Moss had driven in the Sebring three-hour the previous year. It was entered initially in the Nurburgring 1000 kilometres race for Christabel Carlisle, who had risen to fame in Mini racing. The BMC competitions department were anxious to promote her meteoric career with GT

As the 1961 Le Mans works car was consigned to club racing—it is seen here leading a Porsche 904, Ferrari 250LM, Diva and TVR late in the 1960s—the Healeys concentrated on building a new car for Le Mans in 1963.

racing, but could not get her into a Jacobs Midget because of existing agreements. So the Healeys ran their car for her to take 17th place overall at the Nurburgring, just behind the Jacobs team. There was considerable rivalry between the Spridgets and unfortunately Christabel crashed at Silverstone, her car fatally injuring a scrutineer. The Healeys were very upset and never raced in Britain again ... but the Jacobs Midgets carried on to take the 1,150-cc championship.

Meanwhile one of the other Sprites raced in the Sebring three-hour in 1962 had been changed to a Midget by the substitution of the appropriate grille, badges, and even the rubbing strips, although the Jacobs Midgets never got these! Maximum publicity was anticipated for this Midget in the United States by hiring world champion Graham Hill as driver. He was supported in the 1963 race by the brilliant Mexican, Pedro Rodriguez, in another of the 1962 Sprites, but both were let down within the first five laps by new limited-slip differentials. The 1,098 cc coupé from the previous year held on to the end of the 12-hour race, however, despite a cracked cylinder block, for Colgate and Clive Baker to win their class and beat the Abarths at last.

This encouraged the Healeys to run another special car at Le Mans, taking a lot of inspiration from the WSMs. Everything was removed from the rear bulkhead backwards at floor level and simple channel section girders extended like prongs to support the back of the body. The scuttle was then lowered and a lightweight tubular structure built to support the roof and act as a roll cage. The front of the bodywork was simplified along the lines of the Porsches and Abarths and the roofline redesigned in accordance with the theories of Kamm, the aerodynamicist. The idea here was that unless the roofline could be extended to such an extent that it provided a gentle platform for the airflow above it, the tail might as well be cut off vertically at the most convenient point to save the maximum amount of weight. Numerous sports racing cars were built like this at the time, with the Sprite looking much like any of the others. The thinking by

The 1963 car had a similar nose to that of the earlier coupé, with a sawn-off tail that took Professor Kamm's theories to the limit.

The works MG Midgets used a different rear end, based on the shape of Aston Martin's DB4.

then was that if you had to change the appearance you might as well go the whole hog.

Streamlining to this extent certainly worked well at Le Mans with its long Mulsanne straight, this car being the first Sprite capable of lapping faster than 100 mph on the classic French circuit. Unfortunately the driver, Bob Olthoff, crashed at White House when he was dazzled by a photographer's flashlight.

Both the Healeys, and Jacobs, made preparations for long-distance international racing after the 1963 season. Jacobs, who had last raced at Le Mans in 1955, was disappointed, however, when his entries were rejected. As long-established competitors, however, the Healeys managed to get their car accepted. The Midgets were destined for a much more hectic season, though, with a choice of two power plants the 1,139-cc engines with larger bearings of the type which had been put into production, and a new 1,287-cc unit that was about to be homologated for saloon car racing when the 1,275 cc Mini Cooper S was introduced later in the year. Larger fuel tanks, oil coolers and new exhaust

The Healeys combined the two shapes for their 1964 Le Mans car, with a sloping, sawn-off, tail, a similar front to the one used before, and a one-piece bonnet that made servicing easier. Later a spoiler was added to the tail.

systems were fitted and the brakes modified to cope with the extra performance. The 1,139-cc engines were fitted where homologation was necessary and the 1,287-cc units for events in which the cars were able to run to better advantage as prototypes. It was in this latter form that Hedges and Keith Greene led in team mates Foster and Chris Martyn to win the 1,300-cc prototype class in the Nurburgring 1000-kilometre race. This was the highlight of the Midgets' three seasons of racing although they also took first and second places in the 1,300-cc class of the *Autosport* three-hour race that year against such formidable opposition as Hawkins in a special Lotus 23B! Throughout this period, although Jacobs had paid all the expenses, the cars belonged to the MG factory. It was felt that they were unlikely to be able to improve on their past performances and he was keen to try the larger MGB, so the Midgets returned to Abingdon.

In the meantime, declining support for the shorter race at Sebring had led to it being replaced by an event for stock cars. But the Healeys still had the

Meanwhile Paddy Hopkirk and Andrew Hedges were entered by BMC for the Targa Florio in 1965 with one of the former Dick Jacobs Midgets. They are pictured here finishing 11th overall, and second in class behind an Abarth Simca. The bar low across the front of the car, with a similar one at the back, was for a quick-lifting racing jack.

satisfaction of Colgate and Baker beating all the Abarths again to win their class in the 12-hour race in the 1,098-cc coupé. Like the Jacobs' Midgets, this was fitted with a larger-bearing engine for this race, but suffered from a broken oil pump near the end. However, it staggered on to its victory with the sump filled to overflowing!

During the winter, Wisdom had been able to raise enough money for the Healeys to compete again in the Targa Florio. An open car could be used to advantage in this race's tortuous circuit because it gave better visibility, weighed less and with only one short straight, top speed was nothing like so important as at Le Mans. The Healeys had the prototype half-elliptic Sprite floorpan to hand, so they used his as a base for their 1964 Targa Florio car. This was fitted with a similar body to that of the Le Mans cars, except that it had the top cut off and a fashionable, slightly hunched, rear panel moulded into a Kamm-style tail. This was completed with a spoiler of the sort first used in the Ferrari 250GTO in 1962. A Mini windscreen was bonded in to lessen wind resistance.

Once more the trip proved highly beneficial to BMC although the car didn't finish. Works driver Paddy Hopkirk had to retire when a half shaft broke. It was discovered that this had been caused by a switch to a cheaper grade of metal for A-series axles, a decision that was reversed before they were used in Spridget production.

At this time the 250GTO was the most striking and successful car in GT racing, but had been modified for 1964 by the substitution of a notchback top in place of its earlier fastback style. This was a rather illogical extension of the Kamm theory that had one benefit: it gave better rearward vision. It was all rather puzzling for relatively small operations such as the Healeys. They tended to follow the example of others whose cars looked as though they were setting a worthwhile trend. Enever, by contrast, was far more inclined to determine the exact effects of changes in bodyshape in a wind tunnel before altering a car's profile.

As a result, the Healeys used the latest Ferrari line as their inspiration for a hardtop for Le Mans, fitting the result to their Targa car with a one-piece front-

The Healeys built their own car for the Targa Florio in 1965 with revised weight distribution to help improve handling. The round outlet on the front wing is for a breather to the engine's dry-sump oil tank.

The Healey's 1965 Sebring and Le Mans cars had similar lines to those of the Targa machine, although they were cleaned up a lot from the previous year by judicious wind-tunnel work to make them the first really streamlined Sprites.

hinged bonnet to make servicing easier. In this form, Clive Baker and Bill Bradley took it to 24th place overall, although the result was felt to be less than satisfactory because not only was it beaten by the class-winning Alpine Renaults, but, worse, by a works Triumph Spitfire of far more standard appearance.

The Healeys then concentrated on building a new car to combat the menace of the Spitfire. They were helped by the fact that the larger A-series engine had then been developed to a high pitch for the Mini Cooper S. In 1,293-cc form, with dry sump lubrication, it produced more than 100 bhp with far more torque. This, in turn, meant that it could pull a higher gear ratio, so an overdrive was fitted. The transmission tunnel had to be removed, part of the surrounding floor cut away, and a new, far wider, tunnel fitted to accommodate this bulky item. The fact that the Le Mans Sprite had been some six seconds a lap slower than the best Spitfire was blamed on poor aerodynamics as it was felt that the engine power was about equal and the handling superior.

The Healeys took a leaf out of Enever's book and consulted Austin's wind-tunnel experts. They discovered that around 10 mph extra could be extracted by reducing the frontal area a little, reshaping the roof—ironically, along Dr Kamm's original lines as used on the first Ferrari 250GTOs—rounding off odd corners, reducing the radiator air intake as far as was practical, and fitting a full undertray. The Mini screen governed much of the front area, but the Healeys managed to get Triplex to modify some old tooling to present a far more sweptback profile. The glass was then bonded in to reduce drag, which had a dual beneficial effect in that it also stiffened the body structure. The roofline was extended right back to the cut-off rear end in much the way as Ferrari had done originally on the 250GTO, except that the tail spoiler was removed. A massive integral rear window that followed the lines of the roof and tail, revealed a cutaway rear pan like that on the earlier quarter elliptic cars. This had reshaped prongs to support the rear end of the springs as well as the body. Light tubular framework supported the roof as before. New alloy wheels like those developed by BMC's San Francisco distributor, Kjell Qvale, were adopted to reduce unsprung weight.

Much of the technology was used on an open version for the Targa Florio in 1965, except that the old Mini windscreen was retained for better visibility, its surround being linked to a full roll cage along the lines of the coupé's roof supports. The screen was bonded in, however, rather than being secured by rubber beading. One of the problems with the 1964 car had been understeer, so the oversize fuel tank that was necessary to complete four laps between refuelling stops, was lowered and the angle of the rear springs altered. At the same time, the hunched rear deck reminiscent of some of the Porsches that

The Le Mans cars are seen here leaving Abingdon for the French circuit on the BMC works transporter normally used to carry Mini Coopers to races ... with the BMC works MGB that finished 11th in the same event about to take a lower berth because it weighed more.

The Paul Hawkins and John Rhodes car is pictured taking the next place after the MGB, 12th, in the race at Le Mans. It has been repainted to comply with French objections to its previous luminous finish. The car's adjustable air scoop is half open in this picture to keep the engine cool before it was closed to reduce wind resistance when the ambient temperature dropped after dark.

Two new cars were built for Le Mans in 1966 along the same lines as the 1965 cars—and one is seen here being tested at Silverstone early in 1966 with its nose scoop closed to combat cold weather.

raced in the Targa Florio was lowered so that the rear deck followed the lines of the wingtops. Unfortunately brake trouble delayed this car for more than 15 minutes and its drivers, Baker and Rauno Aaltonen, had to be content with a second in class, although they took a highly creditable 15th place overall, with handling that was far more nimble than the 1964 car.

Baker and Aaltonen took 15th place at Sebring with the wind-tunnel car, Hopkirk and Timo Makinen finishing 18th in the older Le Mans model. The race was considerably enlivened by torrential rain at one point that reduced the leaders to a crawl. The rally stars, Aaltonen, Hopkirk and Makinen, thrilled the sodden crowds by sailing past the big prototype cars at more than twice their speed in the narrow-tyred Sprites. Eventually the huge puddles that had formed around the airfield circuit subsided, but not before the Sprites had made themselves stars. Hedges and teenager Roger Mac took a GT Midget into 26th place in front of all the Spitfires, leaving the BMC camp thoroughly pleased.

After such a display, the organisers of the Nurburgring 1000 were particularly anxious to have such an attraction as a prototype Sprite, but looked like being unsuccessful as the Healeys had their hands full preparing for Le Mans soon after. But a lot of money was on offer, and they got over the problem by selling the 1964 car to one of the top club entrants, Richard Groves, whose driver was Lockheed's brake development man, John Moore. Groves was apprehensive about the task facing his team in winning their class, but Moore romped home with the help of Baker ahead of all the Abarths, Alpines and Alfas.

A second 'wind tunnel' car was then built for Le Mans and after a lot of trouble with the French race's scrutineers that involved the cars being resprayed, one, driven by Hawkins and John Rhodes, finished 12th. It won its class ahead of strong local opposition from Triumph Spitfires. The other had to retire with engine trouble.

These cars went on to finish first and second in class at Sebring in 1966 with Makinen and Hawkins, and Aaltonen and Baker driving—ahead of more Spitfires. The only real change to the Sprites was the fitting of a rather ugly flap to the nose as an extra air intake that could be opened when necessary.

Groves then bought these cars to run in long-distance events while the Healeys built two more for Le Mans. One of the main differences in the new cars was that they had engines nearer to the specification used in short-distance races in Mini Coopers. It was felt that if they could be geared higher, these more powerful units would be able to last the distance at Le Mans. Their power was also distributed over a narrower rev band, so it was not possible to simply raise

Meanwhile the Groves team took over one of the 1965 cars (the Hawkins-Rhodes machine), for a class win in the Nurburgring 500-kilometre race later that year when driven by Clive Baker and Keith Greene.

The 1965 coupés were then rebuilt for Sebring in 1966 with the addition of the 'chin' air scoop that was to be used on the 1967 Le Mans cars before they were sold once and for all to Groves.

The 1965 Targa car reappeared as a coupé for Rauno Aaltonen and Clive Baker.

the rear axle ratio. They needed the existing low gears to get them off the line, and round slow corners. The ratios also had to be kept as close as possible because of the 'peaky' power band, and there was an additional problem in that the gearbox was at the limit of its ability to cope with the additional power. BMC got round these problems by casting a new gearbox casing to take the stronger MGB competition straight-cut gears, with a fifth ratio in another housing outside the box and an overdrive—giving six forwards speeds.

These cars were about 3 mph faster along the Mulsanne Straight, and were running well, until first one, driven by Rhodes and Baker, broke a connecting

The chin scoop was discarded for Le Mans in 1966 ... with the Rhodes-Baker car pictured here before retiring.

rod after 15 hours and the second, driven by Hopkirk and Hedges failed four hours later. This car's brakes also suffered somewhat from Hopkirk's rally-style handbrake turns—but the experience proved valuable in that the connecting rods in production engines were then redesigned with big end bearing caps at a different angle.

The 1965 Targa car was rebuilt as a coupé for the 1966 race, at the insistence of its main driver, Aaltonen, who felt that he could benefit from some additional protection over his head. Not surprisingly, the top followed similar

The 1967 Targa car used bodywork more like that of the earlier Le Mans machines, except that its nose had a larger air intake for efficient cooling on the slow, twisty, and hot Sicilian circuit.

Jack Wheeler's 1967 Targa car may have looked like a Sebring Sprite, but it contained a complete Lotus Elan chassis and suspension under its body panels!

lines to those of the Le Mans cars, although it was not quite so streamlined because the rest of the body remained unaltered. In the event, Aaltonen had a slight accident, and Baker had to change a broken half shaft—but they finished third in their class and 16th overall.

One of the Le Mans Sprites was taken to Sebring in 1967 for Baker and Aaltonen, but BMC felt strongly that they might benefit from having a car of standard appearance as well. So a 1275 Sprite was modified along the same mechanical lines at Warwick, retaining its normal bodywork and even the convertible top because BMC wanted to demonstrate its virtues. The hood had a hard time standing up to the speed of the car, but Syd Enever's son, Roger—who had been running a similar Midget in club racing—fellow BMC apprentice Alec Poole, and Carson Baird, took it to a 3rd place in the prototype class behind a Lancia Fulvia and the class winners, Aaltonen and Baker. BMC also had the satisfaction of seeing a 'standard' Sprite, driven by Billy Turner and Yogi Fretina winning the 1,300-cc sports car class.

A new car was then built for the Targa along the same principles as the Le Mans cars, but without the overdrive sixth gear, rendered unnecessary on the Sicilian circuit. The nose was also cleaned up as there was no liklihood of it travelling fast enough to benefit from extra streamlining. The windscreen height was reduced even further, however, to cut its frontal area—and it had to be a coupé because Aaltonen was driving. New, improved, alloy caliper brakes were fitted, but they were not enough to stop Baker hitting a barrier when a spectator ran across the road in front of him. Baker was subsequently locked up by police for his own protection! A private entrant, Jack Wheeler, was credited with sixth

BMC works line-up for Sebring in 1968 ... from the left, the rebuilt 1967 Targa car, now with long-distance lighting sunk into the nose and a bulge for its fuel injected engine, an MGB running with a 2,004-cc engine to qualify in the prototype class, the 1967 Sebring Sprite masquerading as a Midget, and a prototype lightweight MGC.

place in class with a Sprite, but it was difficult to work out what this car really was because it had a Lotus Elan chassis and running gear, with a 1,293 cc engine and transmission, and Sebring Sprite body panels!

The Le Mans Sprite that had not been raced at Sebring was then taken back to the French circuit for the 1967 race. Its brakes had been improved in a similar manner to those on the Targa car, and the overdrive was removed to save weight now that the engine had been refined to a higher state of reliability, with better torque. It was slightly slower along the straight, but lap times benefited from better acceleration and the improved brakes. Despite losing time repairing damage caused by debris on the track, Baker and Hedges finished 15th at 100.896 mph—the first time a Sprite had broken the ton for the entire race.

The irrepressible Sprinzel sets off on his World Cup jaunt with a reincarnation of PMO 200.

Roger Enever raced his works 'hack' Spridget—an early mark one Midget—in a variety of forms: with hardtop and sidescreens in 1965, road-registered 138 DMO with canvas hood, Perspex windows and later-style 'wind-up' doors in 1967, and finally with an aero screen, tonneau cover and the front from one of the ex-Jacobs Midgets.

John Britten's car started life as a Sprite, then became a Midget with Ashley front and Lenham Le Mans hard top (that took in the entire rear section, including wings) in 1966, acquired a more normal MG front in 1967, although it was still moulded from glass fibre, then a standard-shaped tail when special bodywork was outlawed later that year. In the meantime, its wheels grew wider and they had to be covered by spats in 1968 ... a typical way for a production and modified sports car to develop in the late 1960s.

Long after the works had forgotten all about the Spridget in competition, clubfolk continued to use them for all sorts of purposes. This car was photographed in the Tour of Dean rally in January 1976.

This was achieved with an eight-port cylinder head, giving 105 bhp, which was increased to 110 for 1968 by replacing the Weber carburettor with Lucas fuel injection. The new system—of a type similar to that used on the Triumph TR5—enabled a milder camshaft to be fitted, but still gave a lot more power where it was most useful: between 4,000 and 6,500 rpm, allied to a better pick-up. Maximum power was also achieved at 7,000 rpm—some 800 rpm lower than on short-distance Mini racing engines. The chief problem at this time was that

MG Owners' Club races receive massive grids ... even if there are the odd spills. Three drivers escaped injury in this melee at Brands Hatch in May 1983, with Ian Anderson's Midget leading the escape from the tail end of the 32-strong field.

British club events are not always held in the best of weather ... but Steve Everitt's much-modified Midget still provides plenty of entertainment.

Tim Cairns is one of the most consistent winners in the very popular modified class of the modern Midget series run by the MG Car Club. In company with Everitt, he was pictured at the club's 1983 Silverstone weekend.

these heads were fragile, so the compression ratio was reduced from 13.5:1 to 11.9:1 for long-distance races, and a larger air scoop fitted under the nose to give better cooling. This system had worked wonders for the equally-ancient Triumph engine, so the Healeys had high hopes that it might have been put into production. It was chiefly price and politics that mitigated against it. Fuel injection cost a lot more than carburettors and was justified only on the Triumph TR5 because it saved the cost of developing a new engine. In the case of the Spridget it would have elevated the car into a higher price bracket and given it the performance of an MGB. This would not have made commercial sense as the MGB offered more car for the same money.

BMC were still keen to publicise the Spridget, however, especially if a vehicle could be built that looked—even superficially—like a production model. Of the two cars, the Midget was the most attractive from their point of view because it sold better in America. So the car that Enever and Poole had raced at Sebring in 1967 was turned into a Midget for the 1968 race! It was realised, however, that it stood little chance of winning its prototype class as the

Beneath the Midget-style bodywork of Richard Ibrahim's Donington GT series car there lurks a complete clubman's racer!

streamlined Sprite had only just beaten the Lancia the year before. BMC found it wise, therefore, to find enough money to run a streamlined car alongside it. This had to be the 1967 Targa coupé as the Le Mans car would be needed for that event. It was fitted with the new fuel injection engine, which meant that it had to have a bulge on the bonnet to clear the injector air intakes. Baker and leading Spridget club racer Mike Garton took this car to a class win despite losing nearly two hours cleaning out the fuel system when it was accidentally topped up with water; Jerry Truitt and Randy Canfield also took the sports car class in the 'Midget'.

Aerodynamics were not so important for the Targa Florio, so the Healeys had little option but to accede to BMC's request for a standard-looking car if they were to find the money to run it. This turned out to be a Sprite with outwardly similar panels to those of the normal 1275, but it was extensively lightened and fitted with one of the new engines, a five-speed gearbox, and Minilite wheels as used on the Sebring Midget. It proved very fast in the hands of Baker and Hedges before the engine overheated and expired.

There's seldom a shortage of events for Spridget fans, as Andy Mathew shows with his MG Car Club entry in the 1983 Six-Hour Relay at Silverstone.

And there's never a shortage of work or advice when competing with a Spridget, as this competitor demonstrates between practice and racing at Snetterton in April 1983.

Meanwhile, the Le Mans car was rebuilt with the latest engine to run alongside a new Healey SR prototype powered by a Coventry Climax engine. This was entirely the Healey's effort, whereas the money and the drivers for the Sprite were supplied by BMC. In this race, Enever and Poole enjoyed a trouble-free run to 15th place, the old 1,300-cc class having been adjusted to 1,600 cc to encourage an Alpine win. The Sprite's average speed of 94.727 mph in wet and cold conditions was especially creditable because a new chicane and pit lane had been introduced to reduce the enormous speeds reached by the big prototype cars. But this event marked a sad end to the Healeys' involvement with the Sprite in competition. With the advent of British Leyland and rationalisation, the works competition department and the Sprite model name were on the way out.

But there's nothing like a blast of fresh sea air for Robert Beaumont sprinting his Sprite along the front at Brighton in the 1983 Speed Trials.

Plate 1 Everybody's dream of a Frogeye ... with wire wheels and hardtop.

Plate 2 The cheeky profile of the first Sprite.

Plate 3 Stark, simple, and utterly practical ... the cockpit of a Frogeye.

Plate 4 How it used to be ... Peter Riley and Mike Hughes take their works MG Midget to a class victory in the 1962 Monte Carlo Rally.

Plate 5 Blast from the past ... J. A. Tassell's immaculately-preserved Mark I Midget.

Plate 6 Ready for action ... Richard Higgins's WSM Sprite at Silverstone in 1983.

Plate 7 Rauno Aaltonen in action again ... at Le Mans in 1965, his Sprite's headlights covered by protective paper and tape.

Plate 8 (opposite page) Aaltonen takes his Targa Florio Sprite to fifteenth place in the 1965 classic.

Plate 9 What better when the shadows turn to night, than to be out in a Sprite?

Plate 10 Aaltonen heads for another class win at Sebring in 1967 with Clive Baker.

Plate 11 Last of the Sprites ... an Austin version produced in 1971.

Plate 12 For a short time the Midget was made with rounded rear wheel arches.

Plate 13 (overleaf) Reminder of past glories ... G. T. Saxton's Sebring Sprite in action at Silverstone in 1983.

Plate 14 Pride and joy of a concours competitor ... his Midget's engine compartment.

Plate 15 You can't say neigh to a Midget!

Plate 16 'We Buy Cars For Cash'
... but not many Midgets any more
because people won't part with
them.

Plate 17 Latter-day Midgets
became much more luxurious.

Plate 18 Winner in historic racing ... Allan Miles with his Frogeye at Donington in 1983.

Plate 19 Winner in concours ... a superb 1275 Midget.

Plate 20 Winner in modified Midget racing ... Tim Cairns at Snetterton in 1983.

Plate 21 Winner in sprinting ... Ian Hulett's modified Midget at Brighton in 1983.

Plate 22 Frogeye on the front ... Robert Beaumont's Austin Healey Club-entered car on the promenade for the Brighton Speed Trials in 1983.

Plate 23 (opposite page) Clubman's Midget ... Andrew Ainsworth's example at Oulton Park in 1983.

Plate 24 (opposite page) Fun in the city ... the Arkley SS pictured at bay in a London Mews.

Plate 25 Fun in the country ... constructor Chris Smith burns up the road with his Spridget disguised as a Lotus Eleven, the Westfield.

Plate 26 Fun with a Spridget ... camping out at the MG Car Club's famous Silvertone weekend in 1983.

Not that the Healeys wanted it that way. They still hoped to find alternative means of support and built a new Sprite for the 1969 Targa Florio. This was what amounted to an open version of the last Le Mans car, but it was eventually sold unraced and unpainted to an American dealer as it waited in vain for a sponsor.

Throughout this period, drivers and entrants had been having a lot of success with Spridgets at national level and the occasional good result in international competition—such as the Circuit of Ireland, a tarmac rally—for drivers like Poole.

But while he drove with Hopkirk and Tom Nash in a works 1800 saloon in the 1968 London-to-Sydney rally, Sprinzel made a surprising re-appearance with a re-incarnation of PMO 200! This unlikely car for a marathon rally over very rough terrain was based on the floorpan of Sprinzel's last rally car and fitted with glass fibre bodywork along the lines of the contemporary Midget. A works-style hardtop was fitted, complete with three fuel tanks moulded in on top of the roof to give a total capacity of 37 gallons! Four spare wheels could also be carried, two in a reshaped boot and two on the roof. These Minilite wheels were a good deal wider than average because they would be shared with the works 1800s. The engine was a low-compression 1,300 cc and was linked to a five-speed gearbox with a heavy-duty limited-slip differential rear axle. Obviously there were other extensive modifications, including a hammock-style bed to replace the passenger seat, in which even the 6 ft 5 inch tall Sprinzel could stretch out! This extraordinary machine actually reached Sydney in a high-speed blind over appalling terrain, although it had been eliminated by lateness in the final stages near Broken Hill when the front suspension collapsed.

The Spridgets that raced on in private hands were a complete contrast. During the mid-1960s, Enever had managed to challenge for outright wins in 'production' sports car racing with a fuel-injected Midget before the rules were tightened up to eliminate such prototype power units. His car was built to a similar specification at that of the standard-shaped cars that ran at Sebring, but others featured space frames based on the ideas pioneered by Wilson-Spratt. These incredibly light machines powered by 120 bhp Mini-based engines—and particularly one driven by John Britten, who made the Arkley, with glass fibre bodywork quite like that of the Le Mans Sprites—were so fast in the modsports series that had taken over from production sports, that they, too, were outlawed by 1970. The new rules meant that no metal could be removed from within the wheelbase and led to domination by Lotus Elans. The Spridget still reigned supreme in the smaller classes, however, until limited-production glass fibre cars such as the Davrian were allowed in. But as modsports fell in disarray with cars bearing little resemblance to anything that could be run on the road, historic races became very popular with Sprites faring well.

Production sports rules were also tightened up to such an extent that cars could feature few modifications, with the result that the 1500-cc rubber-bumper Midget became competitive. The first one to be seen in competition, driven by journalist Terry Grimwood, promptly won that championship in 1975. Since then the Spridgets have become even more popular on the racetrack, with events organised purely for any model—modified or not. These events, with separate classes according to specification, achieved the dizzy heights during a time of general depression of being so oversubscribed that there was enough cars to fill two grids! This is because the Spridget has never changed: it is still the cheapest and most durable sports car for the masses.

Despite their low ground clearance, Spridgets continue to be a favourite machine for one of the oldest forms of motor sport, production car trials. M. P. Wordsworth's 1,098-cc Midget is pictured here storming the famous Fingle Bridge section of the classic London-to-Exeter Trial in 1984. This event, with fearsome test hills, held since 1910 in the most inhospitable winter weather, combines all the elements of road rally navigation with off-road driving ability. Spridgets need little modification for such events, often only a suitable rope fitted to the front—in common with that on other trials cars—so that a tractor or Land-Rover, can haul them up sections which have become impossible, and a tow bar to protect the vulnerable underside of the fuel tank.

VII
Preparing Your Spridget for Competition

The main problem when preparing a Spridget for competition is deciding which sort of event you want the car to take part in, it is so versatile. Earlier examples are now eligible for varying forms of historic racing, many of which limit modifications to those which could have been carried out at the time the car was current. At the time this book was written, rallies for historic cars were just becoming popular, with regulations similar to those allowed in the modified classes of historic racing. Spridgets are still popular in driving tests, which need a differently-tuned car, rather like those in production car trials. Modified and production sports car racing in Britain was in decline through no fault of the Spridget, again requiring cars with widely differing forms of modifications. But races for Spridgets only have become very popular, with road-going and modified classes, the rules of which tend to change subtly each year. This is usually done by a highly-democratic voting system involving all participants, whereas often in historic racing, cars such as Spridgets can suffer from dictates aimed chiefly at others. Tyres have frequently been a problem in the upper echelons of historic racing, resulting in rules which state that only one or two sections and compounds may be used: the stipulations invariably suit some of the larger cars, but result in the lighter Spridgets having to run on totally unsuitable rubber. So far as concours events are concerned, however, the fewer changes the better.

Apart from the works' cars, which were very highly modified and quite unlike any other Spridgets in most cases, the Sebring Sprites are the most attractive for international historic racing.

In their ultimate form, they featured 995-cc Formula Junior engines with large-valve Weslake cylinder heads, giving around 90 bhp at up to 9,000 rpm on an 11:1 compression ratio. They also invariably used twin 1.5-inch SU carburettors, although Webers had just started coming in on BMC Formula Junior engines in 1960. These power units were built around nitrided crankshafts and special distributors, with a lightened steel flywheel and nine-spring competition clutch.

The Frogeye's gearbox always a limiting factor in how much power could be put through the transmission with reliability, so these cars were fitted with needle roller close-ratio competition units. Fortunately, the ratios were then standardised for the 1,098-cc cars, although the glorious whining straight-cut gears of the earlier cars have remained in production even though John Thornley started BMC's commercial competition parts outlet, Special Tuning as long ago as 1964. Sebring Sprites also had special halfshafts and sealed wheel bearings, which became Special Tuning—or ST—parts. Wet sump lubrication was still the order of the day when they were raced, with an oil cooler.

The science of suspension tuning was not at a very advanced stage in the early 1960s, with most theories still based on the old adage of making a competition car as stiff as possible. With this in mind, the Sebring Sprites had stiffer springs all round, with front anti-roll bars as beefy as those used on the far heavier Big Healeys. They still ran on relatively narrow tyres, with 60-spoke 5.20 × 13 wire wheels, giving a 2.75-inch increase in track. Only the Healey works' cars as a rule had disc brakes all round, even Sprinzel's Sprites having to stick to a combination of 8.5-inch front discs and Austin A40 8-inch rear drums. Steering wheels looked decidedly old-fashioned, too, with a 15-inch wood trim as the favourite!

Almost everything possible was removed from the basic chassis structure except the floorpan itself, with aluminium wheelarches and scuttles on some cars, although others retained the stronger steel parts. An alloy body was then built up around whatever structure was left, with—in most cases—a glass fibre bonnet. The overall weight was generally around 11 cwt. It is quite feasible to build up a Sebring Sprite from any quarter elliptic Spridget floorpan, providing enough finance is available. But the body panels have to be made by hand and the labour content can be enormous, so as things stand at present in historic racing, it is not worthwhile. The same sort of money can buy a far more competitive car for today's races, which are over much shorter distances than those in which the Spridgets used to star. However, rules concerning eligibility

The basic A-series power train, with, for once, lifting hooks! This picture was taken in 1961, but it changed little in essence, other than for differing forms of cylinder head and capacity, and new gear ratios, over the years.

are constantly changing and there seems little doubt that the Sebring Sprites will have their day again, particularly if they are allowed to run with the highly-practical 1,293-cc units like those in the racing Mini Cooper S.

The cost of preparing a Spridget for other forms of historic racing can be far lower, particularly for cars of the type built before 1967 and 1971. This means that the 1275 Spridgets can run in the 1,300-cc class and are far more competitive because fewer modifications are generally allowed. In these cases, the easiest way to give some cars more performance is to swop their 948-cc or 1098-cc engines for a 1275. But should this not be possible, then twin 1.25-inch SUs on a 948 give a worthwhile power increase, especially with a freer-flowing exhaust manifold and a little polishing of the ports. But it is a good idea to fit a 12G295 cylinder head from one of the later transverse-engined BMC A series cars. With the larger carburettors, it will take the engine up to 45 bhp straight away. Lots of other Mini engine parts fit the Frogeye as well. The best thing to do with the early 1.75-inch main bearing 1,098-cc engine is to try to keep it in one piece because they never revved with any reliability and they were prone to overheating as well. The later 2-inch main bearing engines were far superior and had the 12G295 head as standard.

The very rare short-stroke Mini Cooper 970S engines that were also current at the time were probably the best standard A-series BMC engine, however, and were very similar to the long-stroke 1,071-cc and 1,275-cc Mini Cooper S engines. The main difference, apart from capacity, was that the ultra-short stroke 970S revved far more smoothly. These engines have to be changed

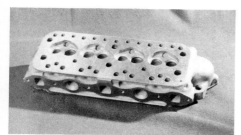
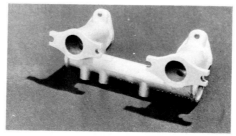
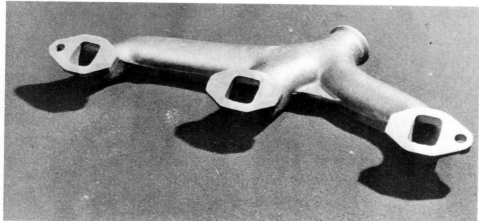

The A-series head as it was in 1961, showing its heart-shaped combustion chambers, with inlet, and exhaust, manifolds.

as a complete unit for the Spridget, however, because they have a number of modifications, including different bearings.

There are three basic stages of tuning for the 1,275-cc engine. The first chiefly involves fitting 1.5-inch SUs rather than the standard 1.25-inch carburettors, which gives an instant extra 5 bhp. But take care that the carburettor and manifold bolt holes line up because the early ones had holes at top and bottom like those on the Spridget manifold—whereas later carburettors of this size had diagonal holes and some even had four holes.

The standard 12G940 head makes an ideal base for tuning, with only polishing and grinding in of the valve seats, with heavier valve springs, being needed for a first stage. In this form the engine is ideal for driving test cars, with plenty of torque as well as power.

A second stage, which is about as far as you would want to go to include road work, involves modifying the head to take the larger 1.4-inch Cooper S inlet valves and Cooper S high-compression pistons. The combustion chambers should be taken out to 16.4 cc, with power rising to 75 bhp. Further improvements to the cylinder head's breathing can extract another 10 bhp with a 731 cam.

An alternative that has been introduced recently, and which is eminently suitable for road work, is the Piper RDA fuel injection. This system uses a cam on the throttle shaft to control the basic fuel flow, and an advanced electronic unit to work everything else. The chief advantage of this system is that it gives very fine fuel atomisation, which makes the engine extremely responsive as well as more economical.

A third stage is only suitable for full race applications, with inlet valves sizes increased to 1.464 ins. A 45DCOE, or the more expensive split Webers, are the carburettors to use in this case, with a 649 cam or a Sprint version. The engine can be over bored by 0.020 ins to 1,293 cc, with dished ST pistons producing a

An anti-roll bar, as fitted to this Frogeye, and an oil cooler, are sensible additions.

better squish effect. Some blocks are thick enough to be bored out by 0.120 ins, which with 73.5-mm ST pistons, will give 1,380 cc. After this it is a question of using a very expensive long-throw crankshaft to take the capacity up to 1,500 cc, although good results have been obtained at 1,467 cc by using a modified Morris Marina crankshaft and pistons.

These engines need offset rockers for higher valve lift, or roller rockers, which are popular in America, a duplex timing chain, lightened flywheel, and competition distributor. A toughened crankshaft is vital and must be fully balanced with all other parts, including a heavy-duty clutch.

There is far less potential for tuning the 1,500 cc engine fitted to rubber-bumper Midgets, as this unit is already at the limit of its development. The chief limiting factor is that no more than 0.010 ins can be skimmed from the cylinder head. But the gasflow can be improved and with an extractor exhaust manifold, straight-through silencer and new carburettor needles, it is possible to obtain another 10 bhp. An additional 5 bhp or so can be found by using Weber 40DCOE carburettors, before an improved camshaft and valves are needed for an additional 30 bhp. An oil cooler is highly desirable with this engine if high revs are to be maintained.

Roger Enever's production sports car racing Midget (pictured here in action at Brands Hatch with hardtop and wind-up windows), received extensive development, but far fewer modifications were allowed by the time the two Spridgets were caught duelling in prodsports at Silverstone in 1983.

C.W. Green's modsports Spridget races on at the Brighton Speed Trials in 1982 with exactly the type of development seen in the earlier Belcher car.

After that it is necessary to move on to an eight-port alloy head with the A-series engine, or perhaps, an overhead camshaft conversion, which was in the experimental stage as this book was being written.

The only competition gearbox is the ST unit, which makes an excellent fitting for the road as well. Limited-slip differentials are also very attractive—if you can find one—with competition driveshafts vital for security if much extra power is to be extracted from the engine. A wide variety of final drive ratios are available for the A-series rear axle casing: a 3.73 from the Riley 1.5; 3.72, 3.9 and 4.22 standard Spridget; 4.375 Austin A35; 4.55 Morris Minor 1000, van and A35 van; and 5.3 Morris 1000 Post Office van.

Suspension modifications are dictated by whatever regulations are in force for individual competitions. Normally three sets of 350 lb/in front springs can be obtained, one 1.5 ins shorter than standard, one at the standard 8 ins and one 1.5 ins longer. Obviously, the shorter ones are the best for track work, with the

There's still all sorts of scope for originality as Andy Waters's Midget demonstrates at the Prescott hill climb in April 1982.

standard springs usually long enough for rallies or for autocross, where the car has often been lightened at the front in any case. The rear springs can either be reset or lowered by fitting blocks between the springs and the axle. The front suspension can also be lowered with spacers between the bottom spring seat and the wishbone. Normally there is no alternative but to use Armstrong dampers at the front because they are part of the suspension itself, but the British tuning firm, Aldon Automotive, markets an excellent racing conversion. This uses a rocker arm that replaces the standard damper, and has a coil spring unit mounted inboard. The standard wishbones and stub axles are modified to take rose joints to enable the camber and castor to be adjusted. They also market replacement trunnion kits to give a variety of degrees of negative camber. The more modern telescopic dampers can also be fitted to the backs of pre-rubber-bumper cars with simple heavy plate conversion kits, but unfortunately there is a chassis rail in the way with the later cars. Aldons also make a coil spring conversion for the rear axle, using what is basically a Frogeye set-up, combined coil spring and damper units, and a Panhard rod to combat lateral movement.

Spridgets do not work well with ultra-wide wheels and tyres because of their short wheelbase. The most effective general size has been found to be a 5-inch rim with a 165-section tyre, although outright racing Spridgets go up to 10 ins wide all round in the dry, but only 8.5 ins in front in the wet.

In some classes of competition, no body modifications are allowed at all. But in modsports, for instance, anything goes so long as the car's profile above the wheel centres remains the same—and then spoilers can be fitted providing their area falls within the car's original plan form. In the modified classes of Spridget-only racing, the cars can run—SCCA style—with only aero screens.

The modifications allowed to Terry Grimwood's highly-successful prod-

Heart of a modsports Midget ... a highly-tuned A-series engine (of 1,300 cc capacity in this case), with a massive Weber 45DCOE carburettor and bunch-of-bananas exhaust manifold. Note also the substantial stay fitted between the back of the cylinder block and the body's flitch plate on the left-hand side.

sports Midget were few: blueprinting the engine (in other words a very carefully-built unit within the maker's specified tolerances), an exhaust system free behind the manifold, worth an extra 10 bhp, a glass fibre competition seat, and some suspension tuning in conjunction with Kleber V10 GTS/W tyres. One instant decision was to run the car with its hood up for extra top speed ... but it was in the suspension that the most significant alterations were made.

The main problem centred on the Midget's raised ride height, which, with the heavier bumpers, made it understeer dramatically. It also rolled a lot for the same reason. Increasing the tyre pressures at the back and screwing up its optional adjustable rear dampers to their stiffest setting just gave terminal oversteer at the limit. As a result, the car was lowered all round, and when fitted with an 0.6875-inch anti-roll bar in place of the standard 0.5625-inch bar, the lap times tumbled as only mild understeer resulted. However, this stiffer anti-roll bar could not be used for prodsports racing, so the front springs were heated sufficiently to collapse the bottom three of their eight coils. This not only lowered the front of the car, but increased their stiffness from the standard 275 lb/ft to 440. This had virtually the same effect as fitting the thicker anti-roll bar. The rear springs were reset to give a 1-inch lower ride height at the same time. The 165 tyres proved to be too wide for the standard rims, moving over considerably on cornering, which decreased their grip. So they were replaced with 145 section tyres, which proved far more effective. Such modifications were legal; the springs, for instance, could have settled in use—after about 100,000 miles! When the legalities of prodsports racing did not have to be met, spacers could be fitted to the springs to lower the suspension, in company with the stiffer anti-roll bar, and wider rims to take the 165 section tyres.

Modsports cars have traditionally shown some very original lines of thought. Following the era of the spaceframe Spridgets based on the WSMs and the Healey Le Mans cars, Andy Belcher's example was typical. It was based on a wreck, with front and rear wings and doors scrapped. Lengths of tubing were then welded into the floorpan—which from 1970 could not be cut away within the wheelbase—to provide extra strength and a better base for bonding on glass fibre front and rear ends with an integral hardtop. These panels could then be quite flimsy to save as much weight as possible, with spats to cover wide wheels. Glass fibre doors were then attached to the existing steel scuttle with old-style external Mini door hinges at the front and Frogeye latches at the back. The standard screen had to be retained, and a four-point roll cage was fitted.

Shorter and stiffer front springs were used with wishbones modified to give at least 1 degree of negative camber. The ride height was also lowered by 1.25 ins, with collars between the wishbones and spring pans, the standard bump stops being cut away. A Healey 3000 anti-roll bar was used to stop potentially dangerous understeer. The rear springs were flattened to give the same ride height, resulting in a 25 per cent softer rate. Minilite magnesium wheels were also used, with 7-inch front and 8.5-inch rear rims, fitted with whatever was available in racing tyres. These often had far harder compounds than those that could be bought later.

The scope for modification to improve the performance of cars in the MG Midget championship is wide as Stephen Earey's 1,420-cc Frogeye shows: apart from a much-increased engine capacity, it features an air dam, rear spoiler, slick tyres and wide wheels, and all sorts of other modern accoutrements.

The 1,440-cc Midget of John Gallagher leads Cairns and John Boness's 1,385 cc example, showing a different line of thought in that aero screens present a smaller frontal area, to be balanced against the reduction in drag afforded by a hardtop.

Barry Rogers's 1,425-cc Midget, complete with huge rear wing, leads Everitt in the Midget championship at Donington in April 1982.

Standard 1275 Spridget brakes were used without a servo, but with hard linings. A Salisbury limited-slip differential was employed with a 4.55:1 final drive. This rear axle had two breathers to help alleviate the common Spridget problem of rear oil seals failing under the pressure of oil expanded by the heat of heavy braking. Adjustable Armstrong dampers were used all round. The engine was a Janspeed 1,293-cc unit producing around 100 bhp on a single 45DCOE Weber, in conjunction with a ST clutch and gearbox. They cost around £850, in stark contrast to the £15 paid for the original car.

Spridgets continue to be build along these lines, although wheels have grown wider to a maximum of 10 ins, and brakes often have 10-inch Aldon disc conversions at the front, with alloy calipers. Engine power on split Webers, with a capacity near 1,500 cc, can go as high as 140 bhp on the dynamometer. This enables such cars to pull rear axle ratios as high as 3.9:1. In addition, where only an aero screen is required, these Spridgets almost invariably run in open form.

Preparing for concours is every bit as painstaking and can take far longer because so much more detail work is required. The only way to do the job properly is to take the car completely to pieces before reassembling it in immaculate order with new or reconditioned components. This is a process which is vital if the engine compartment, especially, is not to lose points. But it is a labour of love that can be speeded up a great deal by steam cleaning the car before any other work is started. It is amazing how much easier it is to dismantle a vehicle if you can see clearly what has to be done. Fortunately, now that Spridgets are no longer made, there is such a strong movement to preserve those that remain that virtually every body and chassis part is being remanufactured. Frogeye bonnets in metal are predictably the most expensive. But major problems arise in general only over obscure minor parts.

Fewer changes are allowed even in the modified classes of historic racing, as Preston's Sprite reveals.

VIII
Strengths and Weaknesses

Spridgets were built with such well-tried components that they had no points which could originally be called weaknesses. Problems that have developed today are almost certainly going to be those associated with old age. But in view of the great antiquity, for a mass-produced car, of some Spridgets, this can be just about anything!

The major enemy is a common one: corrosion. It is caused chiefly by a build-up of road debris and the underside of the body becoming soaked by spray thrown up by the wheels and those of other vehicles. This is particularly dangerous in areas where rock salt is used to combat icy conditions—which seems to be about half of the Western world now. Such a saline solution can cause rust to eat through a Spridget's bodywork and floorpan in three or four winters if cleanliness is neglected. It means that there is not a Spridget on the road that is not a potential victim. How to combat the problem is detailed in the next chapter. But corrosion is also a problem that can result from a car being stored for a considerable length of time in damp conditions, or where it is likely to be exposed to condensation.

The most important places to examine, particularly on the early quarter-elliptic rear suspension cars, are the points at which the rear springs are anchored to the floorpan. Check the rear bulkhead where the springs enter the underside of the body and the ends of the sills. The metal here must be absolutely sound, as should everything nearby. Beware of extensive patching on the floor—the only proper cure for corrosion at these points is by fitting a new floorpan, which is a pretty big job. Should there be much corrosion around the spring hangers on any Spridget, or the rear bulkhead, the whole car can fall apart. A rough and ready test years ago, when old Spridgets were a common sight in scrapyards, was to lift them up by the tail with their doors open. If they were weak in this area, they would creak and groan and start to fold up, frequently with only the transmission tunnel and propellor shaft to hold them together. The fate of anybody sitting in such a rotten machine has only to be imagined, as can be the effect on the steering should the rear axle break free. Such deadly corrosion invariably starts at the outside, where spray is thrown up by the wheels, the centre of the floorpan often being protected by oil and grease leaking from worn mechanical components.

Spridgets really are quite tough as these examples demonstrated on the 'Summer Sort-Out' rally at Bagshot, Surrey, in 1975.

The sills themselves are the next most important item and quite often they are badly corroded. The only good test from underneath is with a sharpened probe such as a screwdriver, stabbing through what might be layers of underseal and mud. Their condition can become more dramatically evident when the metal is seen from inside the car, as can the tops of the spring mountings. The rest of the rear panels that abut this area must be sound; it is worth crawling into the boot of a Frogeye with a spotlight after the contents have been emptied. You can then examine the rear parts of the chassis rails in the most intimate detail. This is especially important at the points where they join the boot floor and inner wings, which should also be free from corrosion, of course. This task is made much easier by the luggage boot lid on later machines!

The lid itself can cause considerable problems from corrosion between the pressed steel supporting frame and the outer skin. It looks quite easy to repair, but it is not, and often a whole new lid is required. The underside of the luggage boot should also be checked carefully, particularly for corrosion around, and in, the fuel tank. The tank is quite easy to replace, but like the luggage boot lid, it is an expensive item.

The bottom of the door pillars where they join the sills is a common place for corrosion. This is caused by dampness from road debris which lodges there. It is a place that is frequently the subject of bodged repairs made by grinding out the corroded metal and filling in the resultant hole with glass fibre before repainting. Such repairs are short-lived and can be dangerous, so check carefully in these areas with a magnet to make sure there is sound metal beneath the paint. If your car is starting to suffer like this, repair it properly. Ultimately, these pillars can break away, leaving the door flapping from the top hinge, which is usually secured to sound metal. It used to be very dangerous for a passenger, with nothing much to hang onto for a lot of the time, but now that seat belts are common or compulsory, it not quite so perilous. It is a sign of a well-rotted car, however. The rear pillars corrode all the way up, particularly around the door catch striker plates, where the metal is subject to some stress (like that of the hinge mountings), and at the very top where moisture seeps in from the hood securing screws on convertible cars.

Use the magnet to check the rear wheel arch lips, too, as these are a very common place for corrosion. This problem area extends right the way round the bottom of the wing and the rear valence because of spray and silt thrown up by the rear wheels. The bottoms of the doors on wind-up window cars can suffer badly, as can the leading edge of the bonnet on the models that followed the Frogeye. This condition, exactly like that on the boot lid, is caused by moisture seeping down the glass windows and finding a home at the bottom of the doors—which are attacked by spray from the outside at the same time. In the case of the bonnet, it is caused by spray blasting the front, and seeping round under the flange which is pressed back to form a vee shape. The metal is doubled back on itself at this point and substantially weakened. Paint has difficulty sticking to the metal and the crevice hangs on to the moisture.

The doors of cars with sidescreens do not suffer so badly, because moisture tends to run down the outside and to be blown free, but they are still worth checking with a magnet because they can be affected by internal corrosion in a similar manner to the boot lid. The cars on which they are used are also quite old, of course. The magnet should be used in addition to detect glass fibre repairs along the beadings—or the points at which there should be beadings— on the tops of the rear wings. If there has been corrosion here, for much the same reason as the front lips of the bonnet, repairs are complicated and costly. This is because the spotwelds that hold the inner and outer wings together have to be broken, often with the result that the panels must be replaced. At the very least they need repairs to their flanges, which is a skilled job.

Frogeyes are special cases with their large opening front end. The entire bonnet, including beading between the outer wings and central section, can be afflicted by rust, of course, but it is quite easy to check. Corrosion is common all around the edges of the body and especially round the air intake and front valence. Bonnet security catches in their original condition are a rarity and they are often missing altogether. The inner mudguards often rust along their seams,

But Spridgets are ultimately likely to be afflicted with corrosion, particularly in the floorpan around the rear spring hangers.

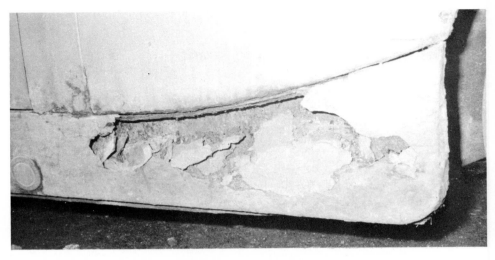

No amount of glass fibre can conceal trouble in the sills for long—as the author found out when he bought this car!

as do the tops of the sills at the front of all Spridgets. The front wings on all models built after the Frogeye rot at their extremities and it can be quite rare to find a headlight bowl in good condition. But the front chassis legs rarely corrode because there has usually been a lot of oil and heat in that area. These legs and the box section that links them can easily be damaged by frontal accidents or the careless use of a trolley or bottle jack. The scuttle bulkhead usually survives a long time, although the lips at its leading edge can rust through if they are not draining properly and leaking battery acid can cause extensive local corrosion.

The chrome strips that distinguish early MG Midgets are less than a blessing. They harbour moisture, which starts corrosion, and their securing clips rust, causing more. The same thing happens to the screws securing the alloy grilles on some models.

There are odd weaknesses in the suspension that only become apparent with old age. The most notorious is the kingpin on each front wheel, which is cotter-pinned to a threaded pin. This pin passes through the eye of the wishbone and if it is not kept properly lubricated, it turns and grinds itself into the metal of the wishbone. Alternatively, it seizes up altogether. Sometimes the wishbone can be saved by rebushing, but often the only solution is to replace everything.

The rest of the front suspension is generally trouble-free, with wear and neglect making themselves obvious on the most cursory examination. Splits in any of the rubber seals, particularly those on the steering rack, need immediate attention, or rapid wear will result as dirt gets into the mating surfaces. The rear suspension is generally trouble-free, especially on half-elliptic models. But squeaks are all too common in quarter-elliptic cars. They are caused by dry rubbers that should have been treated with special rubber lubricant. The quarter-elliptic cars are also especially sensitive to imperfections in the road, such as cat's eyes, and to side winds, if there is any wear in the moving parts of the rear suspension. Corrosion crops up sometimes in the radius arms, too.

The old-fashioned lever-arm shock absorbers do not last so long as modern

A Sprite as it should look ... showing all the points to watch for rampant rust in later years.

telescopic ones, and need careful inspection. But you do not even need to look at them if they are badly worn; the car feels terrible, with sickening clonks and bangs from the front suspension in particular. Settling of the springs is easy to detect as well: cars with this problem rarely sit squarely on the road and ride a lot lower than other Spridgets.

The A-series engine is a very durable unit, with timing chain wear on hard-used, or high-mileage examples as the most common problem. The chains are not difficult to replace. Overheating can cause head gasket trouble and burned exhaust valves can be a weak point if the car is driven hard for hours after a lengthy period pottering around towns. This condition is usually heralded by pops and bangs through the exhaust system on the over-run.

Listen for bearing rumble on high-mileage cars, and if the engine is being overhauled for any other reason, it is always worth being suspicious of the centre main bearing. It always seems to be the one that goes first and it is a good idea to replace it as a precaution. Slimy yellow deposits or foaming in the oil filler are a good indication of worn bores or valve guides. Eventually low compression makes starting difficult. Trouble tuning SU carburettors can often be caused by air getting in from wear at the point where their linkage runs into the body. It is easily cured, however.

The same general observations apply to the Triumph engine used in the later Midgets. It is a very long-lived unit and oil consumption should be low. The only problem likely to manifest itself at high mileages is bearing rumble. It is one of the first signs that an engine needs a complete rebuild.

A significant number of owners have found the Frogeye's gearbox to be its weakest point. Heavy-handed and unfeeling use can result in its unsynchronised first gear and the synchromesh on second gear being wrecked. This is because the first two ratios have more torque to cope with, and are likely to have been engaged at a wider range of shaft speeds. Rebuilds are not expensive by the standards associated with other cars, however, and the gearboxes used in later cars were much stronger. Gearlever rattle commonly came with the introduction of baulk ring synchromesh. The Marina gearbox used on the rubber-bumper

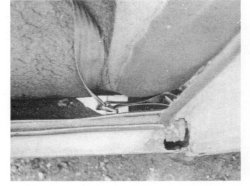 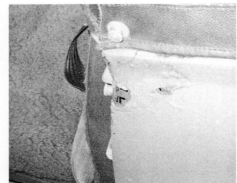

Other revealing shots of the author's 1967 model Sprite, with rust at the bottom and the tops of the door shut panel. Amazingly enough, this car passed its Department of Transport safety test only two months before the pictures were taken.

Rear wheel arches and the roots of the rear wings where they meet the sills are common corrosion points.

cars is just as durable, but the synchromesh on any of these units can suffer on high-mileage cars if they have not been treated sympathetically. If the oil is always warmed up before use in exceptionally cold climates, the life of a gearbox can be increased dramatically, and it is essential to change gear calmly and concisely if a gearbox is expected to last a long time. The rare close-ratio straight-cut-gearsets are by far the strongest and should be able to cope over a long period with any power that can be extracted from a Spridget.

Rear axles are exceptionally durable although they can become noisy at a relatively early point in their life. It is amazing how long they can go on, making the most alarming noises! Oil seals fail under extreme pressure, however, and need checking.

The rear brakes and handbrake mechanism suffer badly from a lack of attention and infrequent lubrication. It is vital to service them properly with brake grease and to keep the handbrake linkage clean and well-oiled. The front brakes, whether drum or disc, present no unusual problems, although corrosion

Spray and debris from salt-laden roads can play havoc with the metal work at the bottom of the wings.

Doors also start to show rot, usually first from the bottom corners.

The way in which sills rot from the inside out is shown clearly here.

of the hydraulic lines leading to the brakes at either end is common. The only cure is to replace the offending items, possibly with better-quality metal, such as copper. It is also worth considering running them inside the car if it is being rebuilt. They last almost indefinitely then.

The condition of the interior, hood and sidescreens, if fitted, should be obvious from even a quick examination. Rubber parts that have cracked and perished in hot climates are relatively expensive to replace and can only be resurrected with rubber lubricant if they are caught at a very early point of deterioration. The interior parts, generally, are not particularly long-lived, having been designed to a tight budget, but they have the virtue of being relatively simple as a result. This makes most interior parts—especially those in the early cars—quite easy to replace. The hood on the convertibles, of course, should be fitted by an experienced person so that the correct tension can be maintained.

The electrical components and wiring on a Spridget are quite straightforward, but suffered from some penny-pinching on the Frogeye, particularly so far as fuses were concerned. It is well worth considering having a car rewired for safety's sake, because excellent replacement looms are available at a reasonable price. These can be bought in the original cloth binding, or in the more modern, and longer-lasting, plastic protection. A battery cut-off switch, although non-original, is a worthwhile fitting. Most of the metal used for concealed parts of the lighting system was of a relatively poor quality, so it often needs replacement on older cars. And the gearbox drive from the back of the dynamo is a distinctly period piece that I cannot recall having seen on any other car. It might be highly attractive from a purist's point of view, but it wears out quite easily and it is perfectly practical to replace the rev counter with an electrical one. Positive-earth cars can then be converted to negative earth with an alternator if originality is not of prime importance.

The front suspension in detail before the steering rack is fitted.

IX

Common Problems

One of the delights of the Spridget is that you can do just about any job on it yourself, without special equipment, providing it does not need welding. It is possible to repair the bodyshell with the minimum of equipment, but it needs a lot of skill. But if you know what has to be done, you can save yourself a lot of money by doing much of the preparation, and the finishing work, yourself.

In its 948-cc form, the A-series engine lasts well, providing you do not over-rev it and break the crankshaft. This stricture is even more important with the early 1,098-cc engine. Even the later 1098s can start to rumble after about 35,000 miles, although the 1,275-cc unit usually lasts longer in this respect. It has more of a tendency towards head gasket problems than anything else, because its bores are so close together. The chief problem, apart from old age affecting the bottom end with the 1,500-cc engine, is likely to be changing the front sparking plug: you have to loosen the alternator to get at it! But bear in mind that a good A-series engine should idle with about 20–25 psi and show more than 40 psi when the car is cruising in top at 50 mph. Do not tolerate anything less.

If you mean to make an A-series crankshaft last as long as possible, it is wise to change the bearings every 25,000 miles. The sump should be taken down at this point in any case, so that the sludge which will have built up can be removed and the oil strainer cleaned. This is also a good time to change the timing chain. Sometimes they last only 20,000 miles, but they break only rarely. Rocker shafts can wear and make a lot of noise, but if you can stand it they seem to go on forever. The timing chain's noise is very distinct, however, and can be heard especially when the engine is idling, and the oil is well and truly hot. The Mini-Cooper S duplex chains are well worth fitting as a replacement.

If you have to remove the engine, the first thing to do with the Frogeye, for instance, is to disconnect the battery and remove the bonnet. That's quite straightforward, but it's amazing how many owners of the later cars complain about what a pain in the neck their bonnets are, and then do nothing about it. The normal 'alligator' bonnet does not open far enough for easy access to important items because the wiper arms get in the way. It is far easier to take off both the bonnet and the wipers for servicing. But first mark around the bonnet bolt washers so that you save time and temper realigning it when you want to put it back. It is well worth getting somebody to help you at this point because it is very easy to chip the paint on the bodywork with one corner if you do not.

It is also a good idea to take off the carburettors to lighten the power train and make it easier to move. At first, it looks a complicated job, with all the linkages, but you can actually get them off together—making sure not to touch the battery's terminals! On early cars, their heat shield tended to rattle. Later cars had a brace bar, but you got the same funny noises if its nuts came loose.

Once you have got the carburettors off with the starter, manifolds, generator and distributor, you can get at items such as the union nut holding the capilliary tube for the temperature sensor, and the oil gauge pipe's connection. Be careful how you handle these pipes because the unit is a write-off if you break them. You may also have oil cooler hose connections to remove. Hold on to the fittings while releasing the union nuts, or they may bind and make the task much more difficult. It is surprising how many people fit an oil cooler and then forget all about it. The hoses are likely to last no longer than any others on the car. They should be changed at the same time as those for the water radiator. I found that an interval of between one year and 18 months worked well.

Life is much easier with a Frogeye than the later models, of course, once the water radiator is out of the way. You should remove this first with the later cars, as well, but there is still a lot of metal in the way. Make sure you remove the metal water pipe on the crossmember in front of the engine in case it gets squashed. Spridget engines very rarely have lifting hooks attached to them, but you can get them off old Austin A40s and Morris Minors in scrapyards.

On the later cars, especially, it is best to hire a crane that winds up and down when you are removing the engine. Hydraulic hoists do not usually offer the same degree of adjustment when swinging the power unit out. It is a fiddly job, particularly when the gearbox is still attached to it. This factor is even more evident when it is realised how little free space there is under the bonnet of the rubber-bumpered cars. If you need to remove only the engine, the starter motor has to come off first because its bolts go through the bellhousing and its attendant mounting plate. Once you have the weight off the engine, it is best to support the gearbox firmly on a jack if you are leaving it in the car. But if you are removing the engine and gearbox as a unit, you have to take out the gearlever and other bits and pieces in the cockpit before starting operations—and don't forget to disconnect the speedometer drive from the gearbox. The propellor shaft should also be disconnected from the rear end only, otherwise it is almost impossible to replace.

Never try to remove the engine and gearbox without first draining the oil. Otherwise no sooner than the propellor shaft is taken off the gearbox than it will decant its contents—usually over you!

The best way to take off the engine mounts is to remove the nearside mounting tower as a unit. That's the one on the same side as the steering wheel on a left-hand drive car. Then you have only to unbolt the rubber block on the other side, where the generator bracket is in the way. The rear mounting brackets are then unbolted in the normal way.

Virtually all the components that need attention on the A-series engine can be reached quite easily.

The engine has to be lifted out at a very steep angle, with particular care being taken to make sure that the clutch input shaft is not damaged if the engine alone is being removed. Shaking helps a lot, especially when the gearbox remote control gets stuck in the tunnel if the whole power train is coming out. Of course, you have to remove everything if it is only the gearbox that needs attention because you cannot take it out from underneath. The design of the floorpan sees to that. The same goes for the clutch, wear on which is usually indicated either by a short travel on the pedals or its release bearing screaming.

Once you've got the engine out and cleaned up, an overhaul should be started by removing the cylinder head, but only when it's cold, otherwise it might distort. Follow the workshop manual carefully, relieving the tension on the securing studs in the correct order. Then remove the other nuts so that you can lift out the rocker shaft. Take out the pushrods and make sure that you keep them in the same order for refitting. At this point, it is a good idea to throw away the by-pass hose. It is one of the curses of life so far as the A-series engine is concerned, and it is very difficult to refit when the cylinder head is in place. If this is the case, it can be quicker to remove the water pump and fit the hose first, and then replace the pump. But once you've got the head off, put it aside for further attention when your hands are clean. But if that's all you were going to do anyway, you didn't have to take the engine out, of course! Top overhauls can be completed with the engine in place. So can replacing the main bearings and piston rings for that matter, simply by dropping the sump after the cylinder head has been lifted.

But if you are up to your neck in a complete overhaul, take off the sideplates to get at the cam followers. Lift them out and keep them in the same order for correct refitting. Then take off the cylinder head studs by fitting two nuts locked together and winding them out with a spanner. You'll never get them to move otherwise. But once they are off, you can turn the engine upside down. The next thing you have to do is to remove the clutch cover by releasing its bolts diagonally so that their tension does not distort it. Then release the flywheel securing bolts after having first knocked back their locking tabs. They won't move either if you forget this point! You can stop the flywheel from turning by poking a screwdriver through the starter aperture and jamming it against the starter ring. A piece of wood can be stuck in between the crankshaft and the crankcase to stop the shaft turning while you are removing the pulley at the other end. Another way to do this is to have put the car in gear before you started. You have to chock the wheels and put the handbrake on, then you remove the pulley before the engine is taken out. The only trouble is that it takes longer that way.

Once you've got the pulley and timing cover off, remove the oil thrower disc, noting which way round it was fitted. Then you can take off the timing chain and both sprockets as an assembly. Before removing the camshaft, you have to withdraw the distributor drive spindle. You do this by screwing a bolt into the threaded end and then pulling it out—and one of the bolts which secured the side plates fits beautifully!

When you've got that lot out, you release the three bolts holding the camshaft plate and take it off. Next you take out the camshaft, exercising great care not to foul the cam lobes on various bearings; they are all delicate. After removing the rest of the nuts and bolts, lift off the gearbox rear bearer plate and the front one, too. Note the position of all the nuts and bolts for correct refitting.

Take out the oil pressure relief valve and check its condition. Make sure its the right length, because it's no good shimming it if it's weak. Then remove the oil pick-up pipe. This pipe and its gauze filter must be cleaned thoroughly before refitting. The next thing to do is to remove the big end and main bearings and check the crankshaft for ridging or other damage. It must be reground or replaced if it is imperfect. You should be able to slide the pistons out through the tops of the bores. Like everything else, you have to keep them in the right order, making a note of whether the crowns are marked 'Front'. Take care when cleaning them to avoid scratching. Piston rings are brittle and will break easily, so watch out when you are fitting new ones. Make sure the top mark on the ring is at the top! If there is more than 0.006 ins clearance between the piston ring and the groove wall, the piston is worn and must be replaced. Use a new ring for this test, of course! Don't forget to remove and check the oil pump for wear in more than one position. When fitting new bearings, make sure that they are located by their tags on each side of the half bearing. And don't forget to fit new thrust washers to the centre main bearing cap. A blob of grease will hold it in position while you are fiddling about. Make sure the grooves in the thrusts are facing outwards.

You'll have to get a proper clamp to compress the piston rings enough to get them back into the bores. When you are refitting the bearings, make sure that the crankshaft revolves freely after they have been lubricated thoroughly—and be especially careful to follow the workshop manual on torque figures. New bolts are absolutely essential. Replace the rubber belts on either side of the camshaft sprocket as a matter of course, because they have only a limited life.

Early Frogeyes suffered badly with oil leaks from the front timing cover. This was because they had a primitive felt sealing ring. If your engine still has one, replace it with the later type, which must be lubricated before use. Engines of similar vintage also had a very poor oil filler cap, which could make a real mess of things in a very short time. This can be replaced with a later type or one of the plastic ones from an Austin or Morris 1100.

When refitting the timing cover, it is important that the later-type rubber seal is centralised on the crankshaft. The easiest way to do this is to refit the crankshaft pulley before you tighten the cover bolts.

Then it is time to have a look at the head. Compress the valve springs with a proper tool and take out the circlips and cotters, then the valves. It's a good idea to replace the exhaust valves at least, because they invariably take a hammering. Clean up the combustion chambers and valves, first with a blunt screwdriver and then with, in the case of the chambers, a rotary wire brush on the end of a drill. Make sure you don't damage the valve seats. The valves, if they are being retained, should be polished with emery cloth. Remove all traces of old gasket material from the block and head faces and polish them with emery cloth, too.

If you have had problems with a blown gasket, clean the faces and lay a straight rule over the suspect area—which is often between the middle bores, where the bridge section is thin. If the surfaces are not completely flat, the head or the block will have to be skimmed, providing the burning or distortion is not too severe.

Once the engine is reassembled, the cylinder head nuts must be torqued down again after 500 miles or you can expect some gas leakage by 3,000. It is a simple matter that is all too frequently neglected.

With the Triumph engine used in the later Midgets, much the same procedure is followed except that it is essential to take off the oil pump first because its pick-up pipe is very vulnerable. The crankshaft pulley, which is bolted to the ring gear, is notoriously difficult to get off. It often jams on its taper, and it is best to remove it with a proper three-legged puller. Do not heat it up, or the rubber spacers used in the ring gear assembly will perish.

Minor problems can be quite perplexing on Spridgets. If the engine is fitted with all sorts of tuning gear and ticks over in a lumpy manner, it may make the carburettor(s) flood. The answer in this case is to fit a stay bar like that on a Morris 1000. And if the SU carburettors leak and you have a horrifying fuel bill check the rubbers between the float chambers and the bodies or the jets' cork glands. The standard mechanical fuel pump on the early Spridgets takes a long time to build up pressure and is sometimes subject to vaporisation because it is exposed to the heat of the engine. It is best to replace it with an SU electric pump in a shrouded place in the boot. If it is too exposed, something might be thrown around the boot and hit it. The early Frogeyes also had a coil that was not much good. If your car still has one, replace it with a later type.

Upon reassembly of any Spridget, it will be noted that the bottom hose is difficult to get at, to say the least. On early cars, it can only be described as an appalling job. The easy way to get round this when the whole thing is in pieces is to fit the hose to the radiator first then feed the radiator in with the hose running under the cross member.

The A-series gearboxes suffer from weak synchromesh on second gear, caused mainly by the large ratio gap between that and third, and noisy bottom and reverse gears. Rebuilding is strictly to the workshop manual, remembering to link up the front end of the propellor shaft before feeding the engine into the chassis. Do not neglect greasing the front universal joint on the early cars, or you will be lucky if it lasts 10,000 miles. The 6.25-inch clutch is not really strong enough, so do not abuse it. When it needs replacement you can fit the later diaphragm clutch or the multi-spring one from a Spitfire.

Replacing worn kingpins is a notoriously difficult job and rarely goes according to the workshop manual. Once you have taken off the road wheels and brakes, the trouble starts. When removing the top link of the suspension, you have to release the pinch bolt at the end of the damper arm first—then you can go on to the big nut. But it is where the swivel pin attaches to the wishbone at the bottom that causes the most problems. Manuals are likely to say, simply, remove the cotter pin, then unscrew the fulcrum pin with a screwdriver in the slot in its face. Just you try! It is only in the rarest cases that you can actually get the cotter pin out because when it was hammered in its threads are likely to have spread.

All too often the front suspension looks like this as the result of exposure to salt spray and insufficient cleaning.

To get it out, you invariably have to remove its securing nut and chisel it through flush with the casting at its base. Then you can drift it out.

The next problem, predictably, is the fulcrum pin. It is such a tight fit that it makes you wonder whoever thought you could get it out with only a screwdriver. The thing to do (assuming you haven't got the one and only Spridget in which the screwdriver will work) is to cut through the swivel pin boss. If you are short of welding equipment, let the stub axle drop and drill holes in the swivel pin casting above the fulcrum pin. Then you can chisel out the weakened metal and get to work with a spanner on the slot where the cotter pin was located. After that, you return to your set of instructions ...

Most of them are good, but they sometimes say that you need special tools. One job where you can get away without them, is when you have to renew a leaky rear axle pinion seal. You are supposed to need a special tool to hold the driveshaft flange while you are loosening or tightening the pinion nut—but if your handbrake works properly that should be enough. It's a simple job that can be done in an hour or two, so it's hardly worth taking the car to a garage just because they happen to have the tool. It is also a point worth checking when the engine and gearbox are out.

Before disconnecting the propellor shaft, mark the flanges, using the web on the final drive casing as a guide. Support the shaft with an old oil can, or something, after releasing its securing nuts and bolts. Then undo the pinion nut and remove the spring washer and flange. Prise out the old oil seal, taking care not to damage the axle casing. Something must have made it leak, probably the bearing surface on the flange, so check that for marks and make good. Fit the new seal with its lip inwards, using a piece of wood at first as a pad when driving it in, then following up with the old seal to press it home. A common problem with Spridget universal joint locknuts is that you can reach the end of the thread on the bolt and it is still not tight to the required 140 lb/ft of tension! The easy way out of this dilemma is to fit a spring washer as packing and you might as well keep everything in balance by doing it to the other nuts and bolts.

While you are fiddling about under there, clean out the axle breather. It's a vital job that is often neglected and can be one cause of axle seals going pop. That results in the brake linings being soaked in oil with further nasty results if you are unlucky. Another cause can be heat build-up from hard-used brakes. That's why some racers fit an extra oil breather. It is also a good enough reason to make sure after topping up the axle that any excess oil has time to drain off before replacing the plug.

It is quite possible to do all this sort of thing with axle stands, but it's a lot quicker if the car is up on a ramp. If you are lucky enough to get it into this sort of position, you might as well have a good look around underneath in relative comfort and do some of the horrible jobs, like topping up the gearbox on a rubber-bumper Midget. It's bad enough trying to top up the engine oil on this car, let alone trying to squeeze a few drops into the gearbox. It can be done with patience and a universal plug spanner, but a straight back helps! Changing the oil filter on the earlier cars isn't the easiest of jobs, either, so it might be worth doing that at the same time.

It is also a good idea to keep a check on the rear suspension mountings whenever you have the opportunity. On the half-elliptic cars, the swinging spring shackles at the back can get very close to the lip of the fuel tank and make a scraping noise. All you need do is bend the lip out of the way, or, if you are fearful of corrosion in the tank, file the shackle a little. If you ever take the fuel tank out, and it's in first-class condition, or if you fit a new one, it is well worth covering it in glass fibre for protection against corrosion. Other mysterious rear end noises can include knocks resulting from the welds on the shackle pins breaking. This allows the pins to turn and you can tell what's happened because their holes become elongated.

If you are thinking about buying a beaten-up Spridget and you are poking around underneath, here's a good tip: if it has been used a lot by a show-off who did full-lock turns under power, and it has a worn-out front damper, the wheel will chafe through the brake hose. Strangely enough, you might not notice it, because when the car is on full lock, the hose will have twisted. This means that when the steering is centred, the worn part returns to the top ... out of sight.

The rear brakes often demonstrate a standard Lockheed fault. The cylinders, which are supposed to slide, have a tendency to seize in the backplate. They need freeing-off regularly with the working surfaces then smeared in hydraulic grease. It is not too difficult to do this from underneath the car, and it's one more cause for oil seal failure if the linings are allowed to bind and run hot.

But the early Spridget handbrake suffers from a curious fault because it is so efficient when it is properly lubricated! Excess wear will allow the lever to move too far up on its ratchet, although it still continues to work well. Eventually the handbrake lever comes off its wheel and jams the mechanism. If you have to sort out this one, don't forget to adjust the hydraulic part of the brakes first.

Further elusive clanking noises under the car can be caused by shock absorber nuts working loose. You should check these with a spanner regularly, along with the nuts securing the axle and the universal joints.

If the steering doesn't feel very positive, the rack might have come loose. And if it still moves when you have tightened its clamps, they are probably bent or cracked and must be replaced. A slightly vague feeling in the steering, accompanied by strange clicking noises, can be caused by slack front wheel bearings. If the car has disc brakes, this has almost certainly been caused by half-seized calipers, which have made the pads work on only one side. The wheel bearings won't put up with this for long.

The weather can actually make the suspension squeak although nobody ever believes me! But so can the damper valves. They suffer badly if the area around their filler cap is not scraped completely clean and bits of dirt flow in with the top-up fluid.

It is very rare for the standard steel exhaust system to last more than a couple of years, but there are things you can do to prolong its life. Number one is to make sure it does not bang on the underside of the car, particularly at the point where it passes under the rear bulkhead and up over the axle. If you can't rehang it properly, you can always consider bending the lip of the metal out of the way at this point. Watch the rubber block mountings carefully, because premature failure can cause the exhaust pipe to snap at the manifold end. The pinched-in endpieces on the silencers are great dirt traps and it helps to keep them clean. If your Spridget has the fuel pump fitted underneath, keep it clean at the same time, and don't forget to attend to its filter regularly, even it it is awful to reach!

You will also notice while you are under the car that the hydraulic and fuel lines cross each other just behind the gearbox. Like the exhaust pipe, they are a prime target for obstructions, and it's best to make sure that they haven't squashed each other. Another curious problem that can happen is a stone being thrown up right into the clutch release mechanism. This is less likely to happen if the clutch pedal's rubber boot is in good condition. While you are checking to see if it is intact, have a look at the slave cylinder seal. It's a good idea to smear the piston underneath with hydraulic grease every now and then.

Major body repairs are quite practical on a Spridget providing they are attacked in a methodical manner. All corroded metal must be replaced by new, but, if it is of structural importance—such as the sills or floor—the car must be

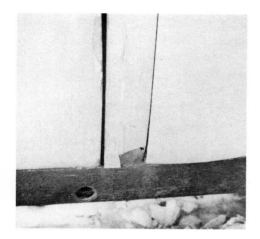

No matter how bodgers try to conceal the rust, it always rears its head again.

The root of the problem in the door panels ... and the sills.

Another shot for inspiration to show how a Spridget should look ... but keep a close eye on the chrome strips.

supported in such a way that the weight might have been on its wheels. It's easy enough to plant stands beneath the back axle and the front chassis legs, which rarely corrode, but once you start removing old metal from the middle, the whole car can become distorted, or even collapse in extreme cases! Minor distortion will be revealed in the gaps around the doors and is very difficult to iron out, even with a professional's power press.

A method that is rarely used which I found worked well when rebuilding my Frogeye Sprite—and which would apply to any Spridget—is to bolt two solid wooden beams from the top of the scuttle to the top of the rear deck about one foot either side of the car's centre line before the doors or any rotten metal from the floor was removed. These higher areas rarely show any signs of corrosion and any holes in them can easily be filled in afterwards. Alternatively, metal supports could be tack-welded in place. The floor of my Spridget was as rusty as that of many others, but like them it was quite sound around the centre section. I then bolted lengths of angle iron (fence posts, actually) underneath the floor on each side, from front to back at the same points as the top beams. Wood might have worked just as well, but it would have been awkward and a nuisance to have had to keep damping down during welding. Four vertical struts of wood—in this case, sections of about 3 ins by 2 ins—were then fitted rigidly to the top framework and the bottom posts. It was almost like a primitive spaceframe within the Spridget!

I then removed the doors, with some difficulty. A lot of heat had to be used to get the bottom hinges off their pillars. But once the doors had been removed, they were put aside for attention later. They would be useful, meanwhile, as templates to make sure that the new metal that would surround them was fitted accurately. Nothing was removed until a new panel had either been bought or made up. If you cut out too much old metal, you run the risk of losing vital points of reference or maybe not having enough old metal to weld to your new part. You also have to leave a decent margin of metal to allow for the inevitable trimming. When cutting back corroded metal to sound roots, it always helps to

The nooks and crannies around the front wings and grille attract a lot of problems if they are not kept clean.

The front bonnet lip can be a troublesome spot.

maintain straight lines, either parallel with the ground, the centre of the car, or at an angle of, say, 90 degrees. I painted datum lines on the surfaces of my car's body to make measurements easier. Keeping to consistent lines makes it far easier to fit new metal, which almost invariably needs trimming anyway—so you might as well work from edges which are easy to follow, rather than trying to create an almost impossible and time-consuming jigsaw puzzle of ragged joints.

The more angles that have to be contained in one spot, the more difficult the repair. So sketch or photograph everything carefully before you start, with copious notes of measurements and angles. Apart from the multiple curves of the Frogeye's bonnet and tail section, the most difficult part to repair on the average Spridget is the area around the rear bulkhead, door shut faces and sills. In my case, the original outlines of corroded parts that could not be bought over the counter were traced onto plywood and new sheet metal parts fabricated with these templates as patterns. This may not always be necessary now that supplies of body parts are far better.

But whenever possible, leave obvious points of reference, such as the jacking box to a Frogeye's sill, even if the metal is corroded. Then you can attach your new inner and outer sills, or whatever, and replace the corroded jacking point once the new sill is in its proper place. The same ideas are sound so far as the bonnet of a Frogeye or the front wings of later cars are concerned. If they fit properly, even though they are corroded, leave them in place until you have the basic parts, such as the new sills and floorpan sections in place. Then you have proper lines to work from, rather than having to rely on a lot of guesswork, which takes longer anyway. It can also help to work on only one side at a time, as the opposite side, even if it is corroded, will serve as a constant reminder as to how new pieces should fit together. It's very easy to hack out old metal in a fit of wild enthusiasm and regret it later!

All new steel parts should be painted before they are welded into place, even if the welding does remove a lot of the finish locally. Everybody knows that bare steel rusts, but it is worth remembering also that primer is porous and is not a good protection. If you are going to take a long time over rebuilding your Spridget—and most jobs seem to need about three times as long as you expect— give the new metal, or the stubs where the corroded area has been cut back to sound steel, a couple of coats of primer and some top coat as protection. You don't have to achieve a good finish, just a water-resistant one. It's the work of a few minutes, and why let rust start, even in the thinnest film, if you don't have to?

Another common point for corrosion in a Spridget is at the bottom of the front door posts, extending right up past the bottom door hinge. Once new inner and outer sills are in position, this metal can be cut away, and new steel let into the face and surrounding areas, leaving the outer skin open. Then you hang the door from its top hinge, with the bottom hinge bolted to the door to provide a guide for the new hinge holes in the pillar. Next you tack on the hinge's captive mounting plate, and reassemble, making sure that the door swings freely in a proper arc. Only then can you remove the door again and complete the outer skin.

Even with an alloy body, as used on this WSM Sprite, there can be corrosion as the aluminium reacts in dampness with its steel frame. Dents are easily acquired, too.

When all the new metal has been welded into place and the basic parts fit properly, you can start more minor repairs, to say, the doors or the bonnet and luggage boot lid on later models. So many Spridgets are being rebuilt now that it is possible to buy repair sections for commonly corroded areas, such as the bonnet lip on later cars, although quite a far degree of skill is involved in stitching some into place. It is a question of weighing the cost of the repair sections and the price of the skilled labour against the undoubtedly high cost of a new bonnet, door, or boot lid. But such is the price of a new Frogeye bonnet, for instance, that there is a lot of scope for skilled repairs to existing ones!

When restoring a car, for instance, it is well worthwhile removing the engine and most of the mechanical parts to achieve the best finish to the body. It is impossible to restore a Spridget under its bonnet without doing this.

Some of the glass fibre bonnets fitted to Spridgets were very attractive and worth retaining as works of art in their own right. It would certainly be awful to see one of the wonderful Lenham Le Mans-style rear ends scrapped. Hardtops hardly ever seem to suffer much damage, but bonnets take a hammering in their exposed position.

The actual painting of a glass-fibre panel is a labourious business if it is to be done properly, because all the existing paint has to be removed. Otherwise it is almost impossible to obtain a lasting, or perfect, finish because the thinners in the new paint will soften the existing paint and lift up a repaired area. A paint stripper which is soluble in water should be used for the best results. It is also likely to attack glass fibre quite badly, so it is essential to work on only one small area at a time, so that the operative can reach the sealer coat and then wash the whole area thoroughly immediately. In most cases, between three and five applications of stripper are needed, which means that a complete bonnet will take about three pints. The glass fibre surface is then flattened off with 220 wet and dry paper, washing thoroughly.

All imperfections, such as gel cracks, pinholes and stripper score marks, should then be repaired. Gel cracks must be ground out to an area about a couple of inches bigger than that occupied by the cracks. The same procedure

Prepare for the worst in a Frogeye
boot where all manner of rust and
rot can be concealed by the normal
lack of light. The circular holes on
the left are for the petrol filler cap
and the piping to the fuel tank below
what remains of the floor.

Severe corrosion around the rear
suspension mountings can weaken
them although the metal to which
they are bolted is still sound.

It is often a good policy to use a
repaired door as a template before
work starts on the corroded bottom
of the door pillar.

How corrosion strikes the floor of a Spridget.

should be used when treating the cracks caused by accident damage, except that it is necessary to laminate two layers of 1 oz matt behind the damaged area.

Next you have to feather the grinding disc marks with 220 dry paper, working at an angle of 90 degrees to the edge of the ground area. This area should then be covered with one layer of tissue and resin and left to harden. Filler is then used to restore the original shape over the resinated tissue. A bonnet will take a couple of pints of resin and two kilos of filler.

When treating an extensively-damaged panel, grind it over lightly after the paint has been removed, and apply one layer of tissue over the entire area. Then give it an extra coat of plain resin, followed by filler. Restore the original shape carefully by rubbing down. You don't need to use much filler because it acts only as a veneer. Then the panel can be finished in company with the rest of the bonnet or whatever.

Serious splits should be repaired by running a hacksaw blade up the crack and then clamping the opposing sections together with aluminium sheet strips and self-tapping screws on the outside surface. Laminate withe two or three 1-oz layers of matt. When this has hardened, you can remove the clamps and prepare the top surface like the rest of the car. The best way to fit a large section is to align it properly, using the aluminium clamp method, and cut out the underside of the joint in a wide-based vee shape. Laminate in the vee, and when it is hardened, remove the clamps and cut out another vee on top of the joint, so that the new laminations are exposed in a thin line along the joint. Then repeat the lamination process on top before going on to refinish the area or entire panel.

Rub the panel down with 80 or 220 dry paper and refill any blemishes. Then repeat the process with 200 dry paper, followed by 320 wet. Never be satisfied until there are no hollows or bumps left anywhere. Flat surfaces are the most difficult to prepare properly, but once you are satisfied, the whole body should be rubbed down with 320 wet paper before spraying. Any remaining disc or 80-grade scratches will be visible after painting—so they must have been removed by the time the body is given its final wipe down with a clean cloth to remove any of the little bits and pieces which cling to its surface.

At least a dozen sheets of 220 wet and dry paper and a half a dozen sheets of 80 and 320 grade will be needed for a complete bonnet, for instance. And it's a process that is well worth doing yourself as it takes about 30 hours to remove the existing paint and about the same time to prepare a bonnet properly. Hardtops take about half this time. Most experts in this line of work prefer to use acrylic paint because it gives a very tough, yet flexible, surface that lasts for years. Temperatures are important when working with glass fibre panels. They can be baked in an oven but never above 80 degrees Fahrenheit as pinholes will be exposed at that temperature, and even worse after that.

There has been a great tendency to denigrate any glass fibre bonnets in recent years, but they are so practical and cost so little that these factors can easily outweigh their lack of originality. In any case, they were original equipment on the Sebring Sprites. Glass fibre bonnets can also keep a perfectly good car in useable condition while the owner saves for the steel item, which can be no bad thing. It is also amazing how often an all-metal bodied car with an original glass fibre hardtop is sprayed beautifully and the hardtop is not prepared properly through ignorance of the techniques needed. Metal finishing, by contrast, is a well-known art.

Once you've seen to the body, the interior could usually do with some attention. There's only one answer if it is really scruffy and that is to renew it completely. But many panels can be copied providing you still have the original. It is maintenance that usually suffers. The spring-loaded catch in the hood sticks of the early Spridgets should be oiled lightly from time to time. The joints in the later cars' frames need regular lubrication, too, and they should be exercised at least once a month, otherwise they become stiff and seize up. If this happens, free them with penetrating oil, wipe everything clean afterwards, and then smear them with 'clean' grease like Vaseline. The top joints of the quarter lights, if fitted, should also receive this treatment if you intend to open them at any time.

On cars with sliding sidescreens, watch out for moss growing in their channels. Clean this out immediately and grease them with Vaseline, or the sidescreens will get stuck. If they become scratched or the rear window clouds over, you can sometimes resurrect them with metal polish. But this doesn't often work well with the rear window and it is often necessary to have a new one fitted. The door hinges need regular lubrication as well, or they may stress their mountings too much. If the doors let in water or really bad draughts, you can always loosen off the screws and adjust them—providing their rubber seals have not perished.

It pays to be careful when you put anything in the luggage boot of a Spridget. Tossing a tool box into the Frogeye's boot, for instance, can lead to a horrible inside-out dent. Even more serious can be damage to the fuel filler's hose pipe on any Spridget, because it is made from none-too-strong canvas-backed rubber. And who would want to see any Spridget go up in smoke?

X

The Interchangeability of Spare Parts

One of the great attractions of the Spridget is that there are so many spare parts available to keep the car on the road, and so many that can be used to uprate the performance of one with A-series components. Almost any basic BMC A-series part can be swopped around on the earlier cars with varying degrees of ingenuity. It was only when the Triumph engine and Marina gearbox were dropped into the rubber-bumpered cars that there were dramatic changes.

Most of the interest in swopping parts around, centres on uprating cars rather than just keeping them running because so many spares are readily available. Frogeye Sprites, or 1,098-cc models, with 1,275-cc power trains and the later disc brakes are quite common. In fact, Frogeyes with their original power trains are rare by comparison! There are a certain number of parts, chiefly body panels, that are unique to the Frogeye, of course. Naturally one is the bonnet, which is becoming quite valuable if it has survived in good shape. The instrument panel is also becoming rare because it was made only for the early cars, but the unusual ignition switch remained in production for a long time because it was used on London taxis, for instance. Land-Rovers, particularly ex-Army models, also used a similar switch.

The indicator light that always shone with infuriating brightness in your eyes came from a London taxi, too. One of the cheapest modifications to this is to cover it with masking tape so that the light can still be seen to glow, but it doesn't blind you! No doubt there is a moral somewhere, perhaps to be seen from the number of times that some taxi drivers use their indicators.

The likelihood of finding a Frogeye's rev counter drive gearbox on anybody else's generator are remote, however, because so far as I can trace, they were used only on some farm tractors.

The biggest potential for swopping spares is still between similar cars rather than from quite different vehicles. The Frogeye's rear body panels are like the bonnet, of course, absolutely unique—but the doors can be changed for those of any sidescreen Spridget. This can be very useful. It is also possible to fit wind-up windows to a Frogeye, but you have to change more than the complete doors; the rear shut face has to be changed or altered to take the striker plates. Wind-up window doors can be swopped around quite easily between models of that ilk,

Practically everything on the first MG Midget could be exchanged with parts from a Sprite.

The A-series engine and SU carburettors are featured extensively in numerous other BMC cars of the same era and later.

of course. So can the windscreen, other than that fitted to the very earliest Sprites, which had a slightly different frame. If originality is not vital, this is no deterrent, however. In the same way, sills and floorpans varied very little in shape, so it is possible to fit new parts intended for a later car. Generally this means only cutting the odd hole, for, say, a jacking point, on the earlier cars. Other parts which break, such as the seat frames, can often be found on similar cars, such as the Austin Healey 100-Six or 3000, in the case of the Frogeye. There are no more Big Healeys in the scrapyards than Frogeyes, but it helps to know what parts to chase, as somebody might have a seat frame for an Austin Healey 3000 and not realise that it fits a Frogeye!

One of the prototype MG Midgets ... using a lot of parts from the first Sprite.

Many small parts, such as the vulnerable rear light lenses, and indicator light glasses that fall out when you shut the bonnet, were fitted to other BMC cars. Again, Austin FX3 and FX4 London taxis can be rewarding sources as they continued in service in substantially unaltered form long after the individual models of Spridget were current. Seemingly impossible missing items such as hub caps with Austin Healey motifs can be substituted with those from the A35 until a proper one turns up. The recent resurgence in interest in the Morris Minor is only to the benefit of the Spridget too, as the spares counters of specialists dealing with these saloons can be very helpful.

So far as mechanical items are concerned, the carburettors used on Spridgets appeared on all sorts of British vehicles and spares are still plentiful. The only advantage in buying secondhand is to save money, although with such an important item as a carburettor, any purchase should be well nigh perfect.

Virtually any A-series engine can be changed around for another other than for those in the front-wheel-drive saloons, which had a special camshaft for their primary drive gear. But the top ends of these engines can still find a home in a Spridget, although there is little sense in fitting a Mini 850's head! There is plenty of good sense in using either a later 1,098-cc version of the small bearing long-stroke unit or going the whole hog and fitting a 1,275. Generally, however,

The wheels might have looked different to the uninitiated ... but they were just the same underneath.

Even the bumpers hardly changed in pattern for years.

you have to use the gearbox for which the engine was originally intended; so swops are best as a complete power train rather than as just an engine or a gearbox. Complete axles can be changed around, of course, although a fair amount of welding has to be done if a half-elliptic casing is to be adapted for a quarter-elliptic car. Differential units are interchangeable between early (pre-1971) cars and later ones, but the crown wheels and pinions are not. The brakes are interchangeable as well, but this operation has to be carried out as an entire corner change unless you are prepared to face a great deal of difficulty. In other words, the suspension goes with the brakes, unless you are changing them between identical models. But, although the smaller Spridget drum brakes are interchangeable with those of the even-rarer A40, the suspension is not.

The later rubber-bumpered cars offer hardly any more problems. Their engines are interchangeable—minus the exhaust system—with those of the contemporary Triumph Spitfire, or Dolomite for that matter. There is far less

One of the first wind-up window cars ... still showing its characteristic Spridget tail-up stance.

With a little bit of ingenuity, the doors on the wind-up window model can be substituted for those of the sidescreen cars.

The last of the 1,275-cc Spridgets, with very few changes from thirteen years earlier.

scope for fiddling around here, however, because the 1,500-cc engine was made only from 1970, apart from a few export models before that. The single-rail Marina gearbox was used in many British Leyland cars, but it pays to seek one made after 1974 if you have a choice. This is because the earlier ones had a weakness in the selection mechanism that sometimes resulted in them getting stuck in reverse. The part involved can be changed, but if an early Marina gearbox is fitted, it should be done first, in case the power train has to come out again.

XI

The Men Behind the Spridgets

Few people were involved with the design and development of the Spridget because it changed so little through its production life; the main ones being detail changes to the body panels and mechanical parts between 1958 and 1974. Even when its ride height was raised and it got a new engine and gearbox, it was still the same two-seater, cheap and cheerful sports car. Credit for the conception must go to Austin's strong-arm chief, Sir Leonard Lord, along with Donald Healey, a legendary figure who probably cajoled Lord as much as Lord prompted him to produce it in the first place! Geoffrey Healey, as first son of Donald Healey, was in charge of the business of producing prototypes, with Gerry Coker as the brilliant stylist who gave us the unique Frogeye body. Chassis engineer Barrie Bilbie made it all work ...

The A-series engine that powered every Spridget until 1974 owed more than anything to a genius of gas-flow, Harry Weslake. Spridget production was taken over by the diplomatic John Thornley, with development where necessary by the hard-working Syd Enever. Nobody fought harder to keep it alive in international competition than Geoffrey Healey and the mercurial John Sprinzel. But it was political hard man Sir Donald Stokes who dealt it a mortal blow and even harder Sir Michael Edwardes who finished it off.

Commissioning the Frogeye was one of Lord's last great acts; creating the marque Austin Healey having been another. These decisions were motivated in the first part by sound commercial sense and in the second by a desire for vengeance against anything to do with Morris, particularly MG. There seems little doubt that Lord, who was knighted in 1954 and became Lord Lambury in 1962, was a difficult person to work with. He had been born in Coventry in 1896, joining William Morris's empire at an early point in his career as a production engineer. He was particularly gifted in this sphere and also ambitious, with a reputation for riding roughshod over anybody who got in his way. His tongue was vicious and his language was rough to say the least; but his aggressive management style worked very effectively. By the early 1930s however, the companies were in a chaotic state, with Morris (by then Lord Nuffield), spending increasing amounts of time abroad and on his charitable work whilst factories were erected in haphazard fashion and decisions taken in fits and starts as Nuffield returned to his group at infrequent intervals. Conditions were ideal for an ambitous young man and Lord took advantage of the chaos and weak management to become managing director of the biggest company, Morris Motors, in 1932. He ripped the old factories at Cowley apart, reorganised them along far more modern lines, and multiplied sales and profits. He also annexed the MG Car Company, which had been one of Nuffield's personal concerns, rather than part of his public company. At that time, MG were gaining a near-lengendary name through the exploits of very highly-developed racing cars that were, however, becoming less and less like production vehicles and as a result not very profitable.

Lord put paid to all that in 1935. He stopped them racing and forced MG to use as many standard mass-produced components from Morris cars as possible, no matter how stodgy. Young executives such as Thornley, and development engineers like Enever, were dismayed at being cut off from the glamour of great international victories on the racetrack, but work was scarce and they needed a job. So they had to grin and bear Len Lord.

By this time, he was treating the Nuffield empire as his own, and it was inevitable that he would clash violently with his boss, no matter how much profit he made. In fact, Nuffield quarrelled with all his chief executives. The inevitable explosion between Nuffield and Lord came in 1936, with Lord leaving to take over Nuffield's great rival, Austin. Nuffield couldn't carry on as he was for ever, and by the time time he was 75, his group had to merge with Austin to form the British Motor Corporation in 1952. Lord Nuffield was the titular head, but Lord was the real chief and brooked no interference. Anybody who dared question him was subjected to the most violent personal abuse. It took a man as diplomatic and far-sighted as Donald Healey to get along with him ...

Partly because of Lord's early insistance on MG using standard saloon car components to make sports cars, their T-series Midgets had achieved great popularity after the war. In company with the Jaguar XK120, they pioneered a massive export boom in the United States, which resulted in their name fostering deep loyalties. It was a market that Donald Healey realised that he

Donald Healey ... pictured at the wheel of one of his first Healey cars with which he finished ninth in the Mille Miglia in 1948.

could exploit, even if he had the facilities to produce only a small number of cars. It also needed his sharp eye and extensive contacts within the motor trade to note that Lord had been left with a stockpile of surplus power trains intended for the mismarketed Austin Atlantic coupé. Healey built a prototype sports car based on these Austin components that looked so good—thanks to Coker's brilliant coachwork—that Lord snapped up the design when it was introduced at the London Motor Show in 1952. Everybody was trying to get in on the sports car act at the time, with Standard-Triumph producing a stunningly cheap TR2. The MG Car Company, with Thornley as one of its leading lights, wanted to modernise their range to keep their lead, but Lord was determined to show that he could sell more from Austin than anything that had come from the old Nuffield empire. So, as head of BMC, he put MG's new car on ice, and did a deal with Donald Healey to produce his new Healey 100. Healey was quite happy to accept a royalty on every car made under the new name of Austin Healey.

To Lord, sports cars were a nuisance, but a necessity to wring every last drop of profit out of parts that had to be made for saloon cars. He was a compulsive amateur designer, but didn't interfere much with sports cars, so long as he got what he wanted. He preferred to leave their creation to outside sources such as Healey so that they didn't disrupt his design department. And so Healeys won a contract to produce prototypes, which with a love of long-distance racing and rallying, was no hardship.

Lord's health began to suffer in the mid-1950s and when MG's sports car sales started to decline (as the T-series Midget was overtaken by more modern designs such as the Austin Healey 100 and the Triumph TR2), they managed to introduce Enever's brilliant new MGA in 1955. This was a bigger and faster car than the T-series Midget, aimed to compete with the TR2, which it did very effectively. But it left a gap beneath if for an even cheaper sports car, which could be based on mass-produced parts from BMC's smaller saloon cars. With the pre-war Seven, on which Austin's fortunes had been founded, in mind, it was oddly prophetic that Lord should ask Healey for a bug-like device in 1956. Healey need no more encouragement and the first Frogeye resulted in 1958, as Lord saw one of the last cars he authorised, the Mini, close to production. Lord remained on BMC's board until 1966 and in an honorary capacity until his death in 1967.

Meanwhile the delightful Donald Healey endeared himself to all who knew him. He was born in Britain's western-most county, Cornwall, in 1898, at Perranporth, where his father and mother ran a highly-prosperous general store. Cornish people have a reputation for being independent and insular, and to the young Donald Healey, the rest of England—or simply, England, as he called it—seemed a far-off place across the River Tamar. But Cornwall's economy, based on mining, was in decline at the turn of the century and he had to look further afield for rewarding work. His father, Fred—known affectionately by his family by his initials, J.F.—was something of an inventor and seems to have imparted more than a fair share of his ability to his son, Donald. He also managed to come up with the money to establish Donald—known in turn, by his children, as D.M.H.—in an apprenticeship with the Sopwith aircraft company at Kingston-upon-Thames, near the old Brooklands race track and flying field.

Before his engineering apprenticeship was over, the patriotic D.M.H. had volunteered to be a pilot in the 1914–18 war, but was invalided out of active service following a crash. He spent the rest of the war working on aircraft inspection and getting an even better technical education. But after the war, he returned home, seeing no future in aircraft other than as machines for war. By 1920, his father—now a pioneer motorist—had built a garage next to the store, where D.M.H. spent all hours working on cars. At the same time, father and son started a radio factory. They were also a sporting family, with a love for swimming and sailing and of course motoring. D.M.H. was an excellent driver, and was soon competing in local events, sometimes with J.F. as navigator. Soon his services were in demand as a freelance driver which he fulfilled whilst he also managed the garage at the same time—a common occurrence in the motor industry.

One of the first national events he competed in was the London-to-Land's End Trial, which passed near Perranporth. Some of the disused mine roads were really tortuous, and D.M.H. had soon found one of the trial's most difficult tests, the famous Bluehills Mine Hill. This event was to provide him with some of his first awards as he drove for ABC, (which was produced by Sopwith) Ariel, Riley, Invicta and Triumph. It was with a tiny Triumph saloon that he won what amounted to Britain's first RAC Rally and with Invicta that he won the Monte Carlo Rally. By this time, in 1931, his international rally career was reaching its peak, the garage run by a manager.

With so much technical and practical ability, it was hardly surprising that D.M.H. joined the experimental department of one of the manufacturers with whom he was associated, Riley, in 1935. It was at that time that he found digs in Barford, near Warwick, moving his family to nearby Leamington Spa the following year when he joined Triumph to take charge of experimental work. At that time, much of the development work was done on the road, so it was hardly surprising that he became technical director.

It was at that point that D.M.H. demonstrated some more of the abilities that were to take him so far in the motor industry. Ingenious as he might have been with some engineering matters, he was even better at recognising the value of other people's solutions to a problem, then adopting them to his own product. His motto might have been: 'A good engineer is one who can do a pound's worth of work for sixpence.'

It would have cost a fortune to develop a top-line sports car for Triumph, so he did a deal with the very best, Alfa Romeo, who were interested in his company's famous motor cycles. Alfa took the Triumph motor cycle design with a view to producing it in Italy, while D.M.H. took their top-line sports car and produced it in Britain as the Triumph Dolomite. It was Cornish business acumen at its best!

It was also during this period (until 1939) that he forged lasting links with fellow competition driver Tommy Wisdom and another West-countryman, Harry Weslake.

Triumph floundered through no fault of Healey's, and D.M.H. ran the factory for a while during the 1939–45 war, before joining Humber to work on armoured vehicles. It was during this time that he started designing the first Healey car with Sammy Sampietro and Ben Bowden. These vehicles were produced with Riley engines after the war, and subsequently American power units, before the Austin Healey 100 made its bow. Despite his extensive travels, D.M.H. decided that the Warwick area was his second home and set up the factory there with his eldest son, Geoffrey, living in Barford.

Geoffrey, born in 1922, served an engineering apprenticeship in Coventry and became a keen driver like his father, accompanying him on post-war rallies. He spent much of the war years in the Army, working on administration with the engineering regiment. It was this experience that was to have a decisive influence on him, for when he joined the family firm after further engineering experience with Amstrong-Siddeley, he demonstrated a distinctly military attitude to organisation. This approach to life served him in good stead when it came to managing the Healey competition team during their international racing years. He was involved in all aspects of the day-to-day running of the business, with specialists, such as Gerry Coker styling the bodies, Barrie Bilbie doing the chassis work, and Roger Menadue as development engineer. One brother, Brian, ran the sales department and the other, John, took over the family business in Perranporth. The Healeys remained a close-knit family with D.M.H. as the inspiration behind their car business and Geoffrey paying meticulous attention to running it. When their last contract over the Sprite ran out, they went on to produce the Jensen-Healey sports car following deals done by D.M.H. still highly active well into his seventies.

One person who was outstanding during the Sprite's competition career was John Sprinzel. He was one of the most controversial figures in motor sport at a time when many drivers tended to be self-effacing with the media. Even the BMC team manager, Marcus Chambers, described him as 'having a mixed personality which fights within itself.' Sprinzel was born in Germany near the Polish border, and with German, French and Portuguese connections, he was blessed with the ability to speak several languages fluently. But he spent most of his life in Britain and is to be remembered as a man with seemingly boundless enthusiasm that somehow complemented the Sprite. He was an excellent driver, but without a doubt his greatest talent lay in the field of publicity: even on his first rally in an Austin A30, he managed to land himself the competition number, one. It was Sprinzel who launched the highly-successful Speedwell organisation, then the Speed Equipment Division of the Donald Healey Car Company, followed by his own firm, John Sprinzel Racing, all within the space of about three years! As a bright, original, thinker, he could be in a class of his own, and more than anybody outside the factory, he encouraged others to produce truly excellent tuning gear and special bodywork for Spridgets. In more recent years, Sprinzel has left the motoring world to concentrate on other lines of business, although his all-too-infrequent articles on what it was like to be a rally driver in the 1950s and 1960s provide some of the most entertaining insights into a half-amateur, half-professional world that we will never see again.

John Thornley and Syd Enever provided a considerable contrast: they were the real professionals of the motor industry. More than anybody, Thornley has become known as 'Mister MG,' his love and influence over the marque paralleled, perhaps, only by the man who created it; Cecil Kimber. And more than anybody, Thornley could be forgiven for being prejudiced against the Frogeye. Although Donald Healey was certainly not guilty of plagiarism, it was almost as though he had stolen the spirit of the Midget upon which MG's fortunes had been founded. It was an M-series Midget that Thornley was driving when he helped start the MG Car Club as a 21-year-old accountant in 1930.

As a result of his undoubted organisational ability, he became an interviewer in MG's service department in 1931, service manager in 1934, a lieutenant-colonel in the Army during the Second World War, before returning to MG's ancestral home, Abingdon, as service manager after the war. He took over sales as well in 1947 as the T-series Midget hit new heights, before becoming assistant general manager and then taking charge as general manager in 1952. Without a doubt, he was one of the best and most benign managers in the motor industry, and it was a great pity that British Leyland were unable to capitalise on the foundations that he laid for them. Had they followed his advice, I'm sure there would still be an MG Midget today.

There was no malice in Thornley, and when the opportunity to produce what must have seemed like an MG Midget with somebody else's name on it, he

The man who kept the Spridget alive ... John Thornley.

Stirling Moss, his manager, Syd Enever, and John Thornley discuss tyre problems on the EX181 record car, which played a part in the Spridget's development.

The man who made Spridgets go like few others ... John Sprinzel, discussing Austin Healey experiences with (centre) Pat Moss, and her long-time co-driver Ann Wisdom, who later married fellow BMC works driver, Peter Riley.

Slide rule in hand ... the genius of gasflow, Harry Weslake.

A man who spent all his working life with every Spridget ever made ... Fred Draper, of the British A-H Spares concern, who was formerly the Donald Healey Motor Company's parts manager.

welcomed the opportunity for the good of the factory and workforce that were so dear to him. His arrival in the post of general manager had co-incided with what seemed to be MG's greatest setback since 1935 when Lord refused to let them modernise their range. But Thornley kept everybody enthusiastic and whipped out the new MGA in double-quick time when Lord could refuse it no longer on sales terms. Its introduction coincided with the greatest expansion Abingdon had ever seen, with production of the Sprite making it the biggest sports car factory in the world. But Thornley was such a good boss, and in such close contact with his workers, that all this was achieved without an industrial dispute and at a cost per car lower than anywhere else!

George Harriman, who took over executive power from Lord, was as keen a disciple of badge engineering as was his old master. In fact, some people say that he almost invented it! But Lord and Harriman saw it as the only way to keep parallel sales forces from the old Austin and Nuffield groups supplied with theoretically different cars that cost less to produce because they could be made in far higher volume than individual models. Without Lord's prejudice against anything to do with Morris, it was inevitable that an MG version of the Sprite would be launched when it was restyled in 1961. And there was only one thing they could call it: a Midget.

Albert Sydney Enever, a pianist's son from Oxford, was born at the same time as Thornley, but joined MG even earlier—straight from school, when he was 14. He proved himself to be a gifted and intuitive engineer, and Kimber, realising his potential, put him in the experimental department. Enever was involved in everything to do with MG's golden racing years between 1930 and 1935, being especially remembered for Goldie Gardner's EX135 record car. He had a kindred spirit in Thornley, who as service manager managed to keep works teams of MG Midgets and Magnettes operating in top-line trials for the good of the company's image even when active competition had been banned. MG's other way of keeping abreast of such activities was to produce one-off record-breaking cars.

Enever worked all hours on such projects, using his home as his office. But no matter how much time he devoted to esoteric engineering, he never lost touch with the basics. He was a man the Healeys respected, capable of tens of pounds' worth of engineering for a tanner. As MG's chief engineer, and effectively designer, he was responsible for all the early Spridgets, with much of the detail development being done in parallel by the Healeys. And one of his young draughtsmen John O'Neil, took over as chief body engineer when Enever retired just before the rubber-bumper cars came out. Enever had visualised far more modern Spridgets that would have helped keep the range alive. But when Thornley fell ill and had to retire in 1969, there was no defender of the octagonal faith of similar stature and Abingdon became embroiled in politics as British Leyland emerged in 1968.

The chain reaction that had led to the creation of British Leyland started when BMC and Jaguar merged in the credit squeeze of 1966. Abingdon looked as though it would survive unscathed as Jaguar had nothing in competition with any of its products. In fact, the entire Jaguar range was complementary, with the E-type sports car in particular as a natural top-of-the-market model in front of the Austin Healey 3000 (the 100's successor which was also made at Abingdon), the MGB which had replaced the MGA, and the Spridgets. But the Leyland truck firm, which had taken over Standard-Triumph, makers of the TR that rivalled the MGB and the Big Healey, were alarmed. They were perilously short of managerial talent and took over Rover, which was strong in this department. The Labour government of the day were also alarmed—but at the possibility of the American concern Chrysler taking over most of the rest of the British-owned motor industry, namely the Rootes Group, and maybe swallowing everything

Two men who keep Spridgets going today ... Ron Gammons and Gerry Brown, of the MG CC and MGOC-recommended repairers and restorers, Brown and Gammons.

else after that. Neither Leyland, nor British Motor Holdings (as the BMC-Jaguar combination was known) could afford to accede to governmental pressure to prepare to combat Chrysler. It wasn't just economics that concerned the Labour government under premier Harold Wilson and technology minister Tony Benn. It was part of their ideology to nationalise industry. So they forced a shotgun marriage between Leyland and BMH to say one step ahead of Chrysler.

Abingdon was then exposed to real danger for the first time. Standard-Triumph chairman Donald Stokes emerged on top in a prolonged skirmish for the job as chief executive of British Leyland. Like Lord, he had a big job on his hands. BMC had been the largest motor manufacturer outside the United States when it was formed in 1952, and British Leyland was still second only to Volkswagen in this sphere in 1968. No matter if you despised Lord, most of their problems had started only when he had to relinquish control.

Stokes was a much nicer man, but he had a task that was equally unenviable and thankless. One of the prime problems was that he inherited a bewildering range of cars that clashed head-on in many cases. He was a super salesman who had joined Leyland as an apprentice in the 1930s, going on to become a lieutenant-colonel like Thornley in the war, before returning to Leyland in 1945. He worked harder than anybody else and engendered a strong loyalty among his staff as a result. But he certainly did not believe in badge engineering and saw only one way clear for British Leyland: he had to start pruning the range drastically.

He axed the low-selling MGC that was supposed to replace the Big Healey, doomed by American safety regulations. But he couldn't call the rival TR6 an

MG because, as he quite rightly pointed out, it would have aroused more hostility from MG fans than any benefit to sales. But there were problems with the TR6 in that it was even more old-fashioned in some ways that the MGs, and he realised that British Leyland really needed a new sports car to sweep the board clean and replace the entire range. Meanwhile he left the Spridget and Spitfire alone because they had fiercely individual followings. Stokes saw the time to axe them both was when his new car came along.

To design this, he not surprisingly leaned towards his loyal staff at Triumph rather than capitalising on the design talent he had elsewhere. First the Healey's contract was allowed to lapse, along with the name Austin Healey. British Leyland was already heading along the path to replace all marque titles with a simple Leyland and get out of the problems of having to run parallel sales staff once and for all. It was obvious in any case that the Sprite and Midget were the same car, so Stokes kept the MG title because it sold so well in its loyal major market, the United States. Then the inevitably expensive development work on Enever's projects was stopped to make way for Triumph's new sports car.

This was the wedge-shaped TR7 that foundered on its controversial styling and an awful track record for reliability in its early years. This in part allowed the MGB, Spridget and Spitfire to hold their established markets. The adoption of the Spitfire's A-series-inspired engine was the nearest Stokes could get to any form of rationalisation at that point.

With hindsight, it is possible to say that Stokes was not sufficiently savage with his cutbacks in the British Leyland range. With recurrent financial crises and some truly disastrous designs, the saloon cars pulled the group down into the monetary mire. After interim executives who had absolutely no influence on the Spridget other than one of negative development, the fast-rising Michael Edwardes (later Sir Michael) became British Leyland's chief executive in 1977. His most urgent problem was to deal with the labour relations problem and with Abingdon's excellent record in that field, the factory was left alone. But Abingdon had been starved of development money, everything having been spent on the TR7 to be produced, first, in an area of high unemployment on Merseyside and then when they had made a real mess of it, in the Midlands.

When Thornley was asked in 1978: 'What did he think of the situation?' he replied:

'My problem would be a microcosm of Michael Edwardes's problem, because he is faced with a situation where there is at least five years of vacuum behind him. I can tell you all the things I would like Abingdon to be doing at the moment, but "at this moment" is the operative expression. To achieve what I want to see at this moment would take three or four years! Therefore I don't know the answer to the question of what to recommend to Mr Edwardes, and I don't expect him to know the answer to the larger question of British Leyland.'

Thornley was then asked, in an interview by Wilson McComb in *Autocar*, why it was that MG was always lumped into one with Austin-Morris and never

The man who had to kill the Spridget ... Sir Michael Edwardes, when he was in charge of British Leyland.

considered a specialist car although it so patently obviously wasn't a volume production car? Thornley answered:

> 'I think MG stopped publicizing themselves in 1935! Sinc then they have just got on with the job and let virtue be its own reward. Now it is within recent memory that the question of closing down Abingdon has been raised, more than once, by, or with all, of Edwardes's predecessors. I know for a fact that the surviving independent MG distributors in the United States have been to Lord Stokes, or Alex Park, or whoever happened to be in the ascendant at the time, and said: "Look, we will give you an order now for every MG that you can produce for the next four years." They haven't accepted it, but in the face of that, MG have not been canned. It's an indication of a rather extraordinary mentality.'

McComb then asked: 'Do you believe the hard time MG have had recently is due to a very Standard-Triumph-minded outfit at the top in British Leyland?' Thornley replied:

> 'Yes, oh yes, most certainly. They were so convinced that the sun shone out of Triumph's exhaust pipe. Then they go and produce this bloody stupid TR7. Though I doubt that that will teach them anything—they'll think the public are wrong instead of them. Anyhow, the people really responsible for the TR7 don't live there anymore; they have either left or been fired.'

So spoke the man who could have saved Abingdon with a successor to the MG Midget. Professional manager Michael Edwardes had to show how tough he was when he axed all the sports cars, TR7 included, in the face of impending bankruptcy brought about by the saloon cars. Desperate attempts inspired by lovers of the marque MG to save Abingdon could not raise the capital to hold out any longer … and ironically, as Thornley predicted later, the Americans bounced back with a stronger dollar and the ready-made antiques that were the Spridgets could have carried on until there was a replacement.

XII

The Secret Dream Cars

No sooner were the first Sprites set for production than work started on their replacement! This was quite normal, because, as Thornley said, it usually took at least three years from visualising a new car to actually seeing it in the showrooms. This embryonic stage had been remarkably short with the Frogeye, fully justifying Lord's preference for using the Healeys to design his new sports cars. They were able to tackle such jobs with vigour and had few of the problems to distract them that might have been encountered in a bigger organisation. Abingdon were also very good in this respect with, thanks to Thornley, none of the red tape that existed in larger factories. So they involved both in producing new prototypes.

The Healeys were keen on competition and produced, first, the Super Sprite, which bore a close resemblance to their Big Healey sports car when viewed from the side. In fact, the lines of the body, styled by Les Ireland, could also have been used to update those of the bigger car. Conventional wing-mounted headlights were used and further inspiration was taken from the Lotus Elite, with a Costin-style wind-cheating nose. The Super Sprite could be seen as a metallic version of the glass-fibre Lotus Elite, utilising a standard Sprite floorpan and suspension. The rigidity produced by such components was used to advantage in that it did not have to have a stressed roof like the Lotus, and could be sold in the more popular open form. Initially, it was visualised with higher-performance versions of the A-series engine, including a supercharged one, to sell at a higher price. But then it was fitted with an 1,100-cc sports racing racing version of the 1,216-cc Lotus touring car engine, made by the independent firm, Coventry Climax. The Super Sprite performed so well with this power unit, and seemed such a good idea, that the Healeys persisted with this project for years, building three prototypes. But they never got any further with the project because BMC would not agree to them using an engine made outside their group, no matter how successful were the products of Coventry Climax in the competition field. Ironically, Coventry Climax were to be taken over by Jaguar and joined forces with BMC via BMH—but, by then, there was not enough capital to go ahead with such a project and their all-alloy FWA engine had been superceded (although it was also copied by other manufacturers, notably Rootes with their Imp!).

Dream of a car for Douglas Wilson-Spratt ... his 1961 WSM version of a Sebring Sprite.

Meanwhile, Abingdon had been asked to investigate the possibility of producing a Mini-based sports car alongside the Spridget in 1959. The idea appealed to BMC—they did not realise at the time that the Mini saloon was going to be so successful in competition—even though they had been forced to reduce the size of the engine from that of the Sprite to 848 cc because its designer, Sir Alex Issigonis, was alarmed at the performance displayed by prototypes. The BMC marketing men thought that they would need a sports car to fill a potential gap and it would be only logical—from the accountants' point of view—to gear it as closely as possible to the basic saloon. This meant using the

The Spridget as it might have been ... the mark I Midget prototype, complete with Frogeye overriders.

most costly part of the saloon: the pressed steel floorpan. These Mini-based projects were given Austin design office ADO numbers because that is where they originated. Design studies that started in Abingdon were given EX-for-experimental numbers, the Healeys using their own designations, such as X and Q for the Super Sprites. But the Austin-inspired, Abingdon-developed Mini sports cars were to be known as ADO34, a basic two-seater convertible seen as a new MG Midget; ADO35, a coupé version; and ADO36, which would have been badge-engineered as an Austin Healey—perhaps on a cheaper plane.

Enever was keen to try his hand at a front-wheel-drive, transverse-engined, project, but thought that the Mini's high, stubby, nose might present problems in that sports car fans—brought up on the legend of the long bonnet—would find it hard to accept. So, as Austin investigated possibilities with the existing Mini saloon floorpan, Enever tried the longer-wheelbase Minivan pan, that also had the advantage of giving a potentially less-choppy ride than that of the saloon. On his version of the ADO34, the scuttle was moved back to give it a rather Sprite-like profile, with a frontal treatment rather like a cross between the Mark II Sprite and the MG1100 saloon which was to be introduced in 1962. The rear end of the Abingdon ADO34 was pure Mark II Sprite, so all the effort that went into the prototype was certainly not wasted! Austin also had a good idea with their ADO34 project in that they linked the Mini's front and rear subframes with a transmission tunnel box structure to make the open car more rigid. There was even some talk of putting an engine in each end! This line of investigation was followed by John Cooper, who developed the original Mini-Cooper saloon, but with disastrous results. The coupé hardtop as used on ADO35 was quite straightforward, being rather like that introduced at Abingdon for the Spridget. Abingdon's ADO34 prototype was eventually fitted with the Mini's later interconnected fluid Hydrolastic suspension, for which BMC predicted a great corporate future. But the entire project died in the face of scorn from Issigonis,

Club racers' dreams ... Roger Enever in the 'works hack' 138 DMO leads John Britten's Sprite that became a Midget.

On test at Silverstone ... the 1961 Le Mans Sprite.

John Moore storms round the Nurburgring in the 1964 Targa Florio Sprite, fitted with a new long hardtop.

who saw it as wasting the space he had so brilliantly created in the original Mini. And, anyway, he had his own opinions about overpowered Minis, that were to a certain extent backed up when Cooper nearly killed himself when trying out his 'twinnie Mini' along the Kingston by-pass. Thornley, for one, was also doubtful whether front-wheel-drive was really right for a sports car, a line of thought that has been backed up by recent developments with rally cars. In addition, the Mini saloons rapidly established themselves in the forefront of international competition in the early 1960s, and eventually the only supporters of the ADO34 concept were among BMC's accountants.

The sleek lines of the first truly streamlined Sprite, the 1965 Le Mans car.

But it was a deep-rooted idea, and ten years later, after British Leyland had been created, they commissioned Giovanni Michelotti, who had designed the highly-successful Triumph Spitfire bodywork to see what he could do with a two-seater based on the Mini 1275GT Clubman floorpan. But like the Super Sprites, this project, codenamed ADO70, foundered on a lack of money, while its predecessor, ADO34, never made it beyond the prototype stage through uncertainty.

As all this was going on, the Healeys produced a prototype Mark II Sprite with a very similar front end to the eventual production car, except that it had an Austin A40-style horizontal-slatted grille and the air scoop on the bonnet. It also had a Frogeye rear end.

Abingdon investigated the possibilities of giving the Sprite more power at the most economical price by squeezing a 1,622 cc MGA engine into a standard floorpan. This was to be the path followed by several special builders in the early 1960s and gave the Sprite a good deal more performance. But the heavier engine did nothing for the handling if it was mounted far enough forward to leave a reasonable amount of room in the cockpit; it made the car understeer dramatically. This B-series unit, based on that used by BMC's medium-sized saloons, was also rather noisy and heat transference problems were encountered if it was put further back in the chassis. It nearly cooked the occupants! Enever subsequently fitted a 1,798-cc MGB B-series unit into the car, which was race-tuned, and used in competition by his son, Roger.

The same idea occurred to the Healeys, of course, but they went about the conversion in a different manner. They were always fond of cutting cars in half and inserting an extra section to make them bigger—a ploy that was frequently used before the war and even more frequently in reverse to make a shorter-wheelbase, or slimmer, car. In this case, they cut off a Sprite's front suspension and let three inches into the wheelbase under the bonnet. They then inserted an MGA engine in a position further forward than Enever was trying, which made it an easier fit. The ride of the car was also improved, but there have been no reports on its handling. An A-series 3.73:1 rear axle proved well able to cope with the extra power and this car was fitted with a one-piece alloy bonnet rather like that of contemporary Targa Florio racers. Lockheed disc brakes completed the ensemble. Performance was in the region of 106 mph flat out with a 9-second 0–60 time, but this promising project was killed by BMC because they realised that it was really only an alternative to the MGB—which was introduced in 1962—and they were already committed to tooling for that. Triumph eventually produced a similar car, the GT6, with a six-cylinder engine in the Spitfire's chassis.

The next Spridget prototypes with which the Healeys were associated were

The 1967 Le Mans Sprite, driven by Andrew Hedges and Clive Baker in all its glory at the London Motor Show later that year.

Targa Florio Sprite rebuild for Sebring ... the auxilliary lights were later let into the nose.

production versions of the Sebring and Le Mans coupés in 1965. But the costs of tooling for these short production run cars would have made their selling price too high in BMC's opinion.

The accountants were keener on a car that could be produced in larger quantities, because the racing cars' space frames needed skilled labour. Once more, they decided to use their design facilities to the full by commissioning three separate prototypes. Austin would produce a front-wheel-drive Spridget replacement, Enever would build a Spridget with Hydrolastic suspension, and the Healeys would make a car with Hydrolastic suspension and a transverse A-series engine mounted at the back. This would be based on the Austin 1100 saloon, which had become Britain's best-selling car. Austin's prototype was rather like a restyled 1100, and Enever's simply an ADO34 conversion, but the Healey was far more interesting. It was called WAEC for 'wheel at each corner,' a characteristic of the 1100 floorpan. A 1,275-cc Cooper power train was mounted in its subframe at the back, devoid of steering, of course, with a similar subframe at the front, complete with steering, but devoid of engine and transmission. So far, so conventional. But it was the body that was amazing. An initial design study by Pininfarina had made it like that of the Alfa Romeo Duetto, based in turn on the sensational Disco Volante racing sports cars of the early 1950s. But by the time it appeared in the metal, it had become stubbier. This was in keeping with the Austin floorpan, but it was the top that was sensational.

Four years earlier, Triumph had introduced a novel hardtop for their TR4 with the rear end made up of a rigid roll cage, linked to the windscreen by a detachable canvas cover. At the same time, some sports racing cars had roll cages incorporated in such a way that they looked like truncated roofs; Porsche were a notable exponent of this open top system on some of their Targa Florio cars and subsequently adapted the Triumph design for their 911 Targa range in

It might have been a Spridget ... Syd Enever's prototype based on the MG1100 saloon.

1966. But the Healey WAEC predated this by a few months and had the benefit of a novel and very effective form of ventilation.

Their rear window—in glass for the best visibility—could be wound up and down by an electric motor, like that fitted in some American estate cars. The Triumph's 'Surrey'-style canvas top could be removed to make it an open car, while, with the back window up, the occupants were protected from draughts round the backs of their necks; but with the window down and the top off, it was

One man's dream of a super Spridget ... the Westfield.

practically an open car! It was all Donald Healey's idea, apparently, and it also made the WAEC a lot stiffer, with added protection for those inside. Engine cooling problems were alleviated by the use of a Porsche-style intake fan, and with cheap new disc brakes all round, the WAEC was potentially the best replacement for the Spridget to date. But it represented such a dramatic change that BMC were put off.

The disconsolate Healeys then had to be content with a Mini-Cooper 1275S-engined version of the Sprite to see off a possible threat from the new Honda S800 sports car. This prototype was killed because it was nearly as fast the MGB!

Meanwhile, the Pininfarina lines reappeared on a stunningly-pretty Abingdon prototype, the EX234, that could have been an MGD—to replace the MGB and the six-cylinder MGC—or indeed a new Spridget with an A-series engine. It was about the same size as the MGB, except that it had an 87-inch wheelbase instead of 91, two-plus-two configuration as in the MGB GT, and all independent suspension—which both Enever and the Healeys had wanted for a long time. Wishbones were used at the front with trailing arms and a chassis-mounted final drive at the back. Hydolastic suspension was used all round and the result bore a certain resemblance to that of the Fiat Spider which was to become so successful in the Spridget market. But BMC were in the throes of the merger that led to British Leyland and the project was shelved to gather dust for all time. The decision not to go ahead with it was as heart-breaking to Abingdon as the shelving of the MGA prototype had been in 1952.

The last of the prototypes that could conceivably have become a Spridget was a car designed under Enever's aegis, but codenamed ADO21. IT was a mid-engined wedge-shaped machine that would have taken the Austin Maxi 1,750-cc engine and gearbox as its basic unit, or maybe larger and smaller British Leyland power trains. ADO21 used de Dion rear suspension and a fuel tank between the engine and the passenger compartment to counter possible US safety legislation, with the MacPherson strut front suspension that was one of the best parts of Lotus and Ford design. Much of its influence extended to the TR7 that Triumph produced, but it looked very much like a Fiat X1/9 that was to become the best-seller in this market. If only ...

XIII

The Spridget Clubs

Spridget owners have a tremendous advantage over other marque enthusiasts. They can, if they so wish, belong to worldwide clubs for either Austin Healey or MG owners, or both. The MG Car Club is the oldest-established of these organisations, having been founded by John Thornley among others in 1930. For years it was the only one of its kind in the field and became the biggest marque club in the world, thanks to the constant encouragement Thornley at Abingdon and equally-dedicated efforts of many other members.

Such was the success of this enterprise, that several other manufacturers investigated the possibility of how they could capitalise on such enthusiasm. But generally they had only commercial interests at heart, viewing any owners' club as a way to sell more accessories through a useful mailing list. They would even offer free trips to Europe for American members if they bought a car at the factory gates, which worked out at about the same price (when shipping was considered) as buying one in California. A good idea, but one with profit foremost in the manufacturers' mind. The MG Car Club was never like that, being organised purely with the members' interest in mind.

A Healey Drivers' Club was formed in 1955, and when production of the Big Healey was transferred to Abingdon in 1957, Thornley suggested that it should be run along the lines of the MG Car Club, which had offices within the factory. Nobody could object—the MG Car Club was so successful Healey owners were given a lot of space in the MG Car Club's magazine, *Safety Fast*, and shared their offices. With the inspiration of Thornley and the help of men such as Peter Browning and Les Needham, the club thrived despite a certain amount of bickering between supporters of the Big Healey and the Sprite. They have always tended to squabble in some areas.

As interest in the early Healeys declined, the Austin Healey Club was formed in 1961 by combining the well-established Healey Drivers' Club with the Southern Counties Sprite Club. Peter Browning became the first general secretary and did much to unify the Big Healey and Sprite factions, organising numerous meetings, film shows, forums and so on, with works drivers and personalities in frequent attendance. Club racing was also very popular. The founder centres were soon joined by the Northern Sprite Group and the Eastern

Club get-togethers are ideal for Spridget owners.

There's always a concours for the truly gleaming cars.

Sprite Group. Attempts were made to persuade the Scottish Sprite Group to join the rapidly growing Austin Healey Club of Great Britain, but they remained aloof and eventually disbanded. The Healey Drivers' Club then became the Midlands Centre and the Sprite clubs the Southern Northern and Eastern Centres. Meanwhile, the MG Car Club continued, with centres throughout the world, catering for members with any model.

Inevitably, the Austin Healey Club regrouped in the same way with the same sort of thing happening in America, except that groups were called

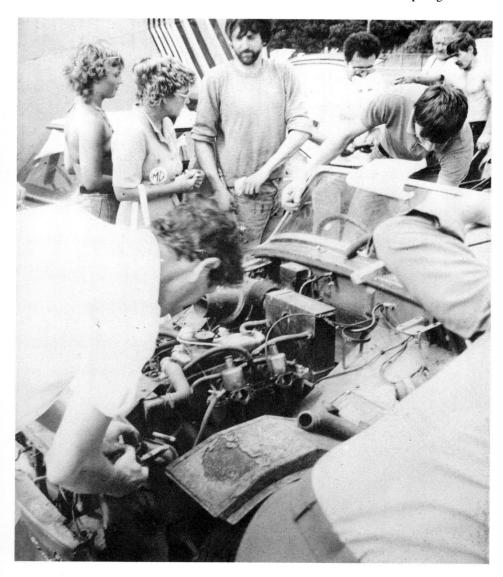

Whatever is happening to this relic of a Frogeye at an MG Owners' Club national day is open to speculation!

chapters. They had to be organised on a regional basis because of the vast distances between members.

But from the MG side, it was not until John Thornley had to retire through ill health that the MG Car Club was challenged. Business consultant Roche Bentley started the MG Owners' Club in 1973 with his wife, Tricia. Within six years membership had risen to more than 8,000, with a roll now standing at 38,000 to make it the biggest in the world. His club's great success was almost certainly due to the fact that it has been organised professionally on a full time basis with the owners' interest at heart—and particularly those of people who own old, and sometimes struggling, cars.

The MG Car Club survives with unabated enthusiasm and a substantial proportion of dual membership with the MG Owners' Club, by providing the established mixture of immaculately-organised race meetings, hill climbs, rallies, driving tests and trials besides well-attended club meetings, affectionately known as 'noggins and natters' at hostelries throughout the world. A variety of social events, such as dinners, dances and film shows, are organised, along with concours. Their summer Silverstone weekend is the highlight of their year with racing one day and concours the next.

But they have always tended to keep a lower profile and the MG Owners' Club has risen to such a large membership by catering for all these interests—although the competition side is in much lower profile—and especially those concerned with spare parts and the problems of running cars such as Spridgets. One of the cornerstones of Roche Bentley's philosophy has been to run democratic schemes to monitor the performance of recommended specialists, besides providing a magazine called *Enjoying MG* that embraces all forms of interest. The addresses to contact are: MG Car Club, 67 Wide Bargate, Boston, Lincs, and MG Owners' Club, Station Road, Swavesey, Lincs. They can also advise on addresses and contacts for other clubs worldwide, which tend to change their addresses frequently because of voluntary—but no less enthusiastic—organisation.

And then there's always the racing...

XIV
Your Spridget Logbook

Austin Healey Sprite

48,999 made between May 1958 and May 1961, chassis numbers H-AN5-501 to H-AN5-50116.

Engine

Four-cylinder, CUBIC CAPACITY 948; BORE AND STROKE 62.94 mm × 76.2 mm; MAX POWER 42.5 bhp at 5,000 rpm; MAX TORQUE 52 lb/ft at 3,300 rpm.

Chassis

WEIGHT (unladen) 1,466 lb; WHEELBASE 6 ft 8 ins; FRONT TRACK 3 ft 9.75 ins; REAR TRACK 3 ft 8.75 ins; LENGTH 11 ft (11 ft 5 ins with front bumper); WIDTH 4 ft 5.25 ins; HEIGHT (with hood up) 4 ft 1.75 ins; FRONT SUSPENSION Independent, coil springs, wishbones, lever-arm hydraulic dampers; REAR SUSPENSION live axle, quarter-elliptic leaf springs, lever-arm dampers; BRAKES Lockheed hydraulic 7-inch drums; GEARBOX four-speed (overall ratios)—with 4.22:1 axle—4.22, 5.96, 10.02, 15.31, reverse 19.62; STEERING rack and pinion; WHEELS AND TYRES 5.20—13, pressed steel, tubeless.

Austin Healey Sprite Mark II, MG Midget

20,360 Sprites built between May 1961 and October 1962, chassis numbers H-AN6-101 to H-AN6-24731.

16,080 Midgets built between May 1961 and October 1962, chassis numbers G-AN101101 to G-AN1016183.

Engine

As earlier Sprite except 46 bhp.

Chassis

As Sprite Mark I except WEIGHT (unladen) 1,525 lb; GEARBOX (overall ratios) 4.22, 5.95, 8.1, 13.5, reverse 17.34; BRAKES 8.25-inch Lockheed disc front; WHEELS Wire optional

Austin Healey Sprite Mark II (1100), MG Midget (1100)

11,215 Sprites built between October 1962 and March 1964, chassis numbers H-AN7-24732 to H-AN7-38828.
9,601 Midgets built between October 1962 and March 1964, chassis numbers G-AN2-16184 to G-AN2-25787.

Engine

Four-cylinder, CUBIC CAPACITY 1,098; BORE AND STROKE 64.58 mm × 83.72 mm; MAX POWER 55 bhp at 5,500 rpm; MAX TORQUE 61 lb/ft at 2,500 rpm.

Chassis

As earlier Sprite and Midget.

Austin Healey Sprite Mark III, MG Midget Mark II

25,906 Sprites build between March 1964 and October 1966, chassis numbers H-AN8-38829 to H-AN8-64734.
26,601 Midgets built between March 1964 and October 1966, chassis numbers G-AN3-25788 to G-AN3-52389.

Engine

As earlier 1100 except 59 bhp at 5,750 rpm.

Chassis

As earlier 1100 except half-elliptic rear springs.

Austin Healey Sprite Mark IV, MG Midget Mark III

20,479 Sprites built between October 1966 and October 1969, chassis numbers H-AN9-64735 to H-AN9-85286.
22,497 Midgets built between October 1966 and October 1969, chassis numbers G-AN4-52390 to G-AN4-74885.

Engine

Four-cylinder, CUBIC CAPACITY 1,275; BORE AND STROKE 70.61 mm × 81.28 mm; MAX POWER 64 bhp at 6,000 rpm; MAX TORQUE 72 lb/ft at 3,000 rpm.

Chassis

As earlier 1100 except gear ratios (overall) from 1968—with 3.9:1 rear axle—3.9, 5.3, 7.49, 12.48, reverse 16.03.

Austin Healey Sprite Mark V, MG Midget Mark IV, Austin Sprite

1,292 Austin Healey Sprites built between October 1969 and December 1970, chassis numbers H-AN10-85287 to H-AN10-86803.
77,878 Midgets built between October 1969 and October 1974, chassis

numbers G-AN5-74886 to G-AN5-153920.

1,022 Austin Sprites built between January 1971 and July 1971, chass numbers A-AN10-86804 to A-AN10-87824.

MG Midget

73,899 built between October 1974 and November 1980, chassis numbers G-AN6-154101 to G-AN6-229526.

Engine

Four-cylinder, CUBIC CAPACITY 1,493; BORE AND STROKE 73.7 mm × 87.5 mm; MAX POWER (non-US) 65 bhp at 6,000 rpm, (US) 51 bhp at 5,000 rpm; MAX TORQUE 76.5 lb/ft at 3,000 rpm.

Chassis

WEIGHT (unladen) 1,720 lb; LENGTH 11 ft 9 ins; GEARBOX four-speed (overall ratios)—with 3.9:1 rear axle—3.9, 5.58, 8.19, 13.3, reverse 14.63; with 3.78:1 rear axle from September 1977: 3.72, 5.32, 7.85, 12.69, reverse 13.95.

Index

Index of Illustrations

Picture Acknowledgements

The author is grateful to the following organisations and photographers for allowing their pictures to be used:

British Leyland Heritage Limited 2, 3 bottom, 4 top, 9 top, 9 bottom, 10, 11, 12, 13, 14 bottom, 15, 16 top, 17 bottom, 18 top left, 18 top right, 20, 28 top, 28 bottom, 30 top, 30 bottom, 31, 32, 33 top, 33 bottom, 34 bottom, 35, 36 top, 36 bottom, 37 top, 37 bottom, 38 top, 46, 47 bottom, 51, 52 top, 64 bottom, 70 top, 71 top, 71 bottom, 72 top, 75 top left, 75 top right, 77, 79, 80, 81 top, 81 bottom, 83, 122 top, 122 middle, 122 bottom, 124, 125 top, 125 bottom, 126, 129 top, 132 top, 142, 143 top left, 143 top right, 143 bottom, 155, 159, 162 top, 163 bottom, 170, 177 bottom, 178 top, 179, 180 top, 180 bottom, 187 bottom, 194 bottom, 198, 199

Daily Express 191
Emerson, Bill 119
Hilton Press Services cover, plates 1, 2, 3, 5, 6, 9, 11, 12, 13, 14, 15, 16, 17, 18, 19, 20, 21, 22, 23, 24, 25, 26; pages 4 bottom, 5, 6, 14 top, 18 bottom, 19, 21, top, 22, 23, 24, 29 top, 29 bottom, 34 top, 38 middle, 38 bottom, 40, 41 top, 41 bottom, 42, 45 top, 45 bottom, 47 top, 48, 49, 55, 64 top, 69, 89, 90 top, 90 middle, 90 bottom, 91, 93 top, 93 bottom, 94, 95, 96, 98, 99, 100, 103, 104, 105, 106, 107, 111 top, 111 bottom, 135 bottom, 136 top, 137 top, 137 bottom, 138 top, 138 bottom, 140, 144, 145 bottom, 146 top, 146 bottom, 147, 149 top, 149 middle, 149 bottom, 150, 153, 154, 156 top left, 156 top right, 156 bottom, 157 top, 157 middle, 158, 166, 169 top left, 169 top right, 169 middle, 169 bottom, 171 top, 173, 174 top, 174 middle, 174 bottom, 175, 181 top, 181 middle, 181 bottom, 183, 187 top, 188 bottom left, 188 bottom right, 194 top, 200 top, 200 bottom 201, 204 top, 204 bottom, 205, 206

London Art-Technical plates 4, 7, 8, 10; pages 21 bottom, 25, 26, 52 bottom, 53, 54 top, 54 middle, 54 bottom, 56, 58, 61, 62, 63, 67, 68, 70 bottom, 72 bottom, 73, 74, 75 bottom, 78 top, 78 bottom, 84, 97, 109, 110, 112, 113, 114, 115 top, 115 bottom, 116 top, 116 bottom, 117, 120, 121 top, 121 bottom, 123, 127 top, 127 bottom, 128, 129 bottom, 130 top, 130 bottom, 131, 132 bottom, 133 top, 133 middle, 133 bottom, 134 top, 134 second picture, 133 third, 133 bottom, 145 top, 178 bottom, 195, 196 top, 196 bottom, 197 bottom

Skilleter, Paul 190
Temple Press 3 top, 60, 188 top
Young, Robert 135 top, 152